Symbols and Dances

Symbols
and
Dances

*

Sermons by
Michael Stancliffe

*

First published in Great Britain 1986
Second impression 1987
SPCK
Holy Trinity Church
Marylebone Road
London NW1 4DU

Acknowledgements

Verses from 'Lord of the Dance' by Sydney Carter are copyright
© Stainer & Bell Ltd, and are reprinted by permission

Extracts from *The Common Stream* by Rowland Parker are
reprinted by permission of Collins Publishers.

The extract from the Introduction by Tony Tanner to
Mansfield Park by Jane Austen is reprinted by permission of
Penguin Books Ltd. Copyright © Tony Tanner 1966.

British Library Cataloguing in Publication Data

Stancliffe, Michael
    Symbols and dances : sermons.
    1. Church of England — Sermons
    I. Title
    252'.03   BX5133

ISBN 0-281-04252-7

Typeset by Pioneer, Perthshire
Printed in Great Britain by
Whitstable Litho Ltd, Whitstable, Kent

Contents

*

Foreword

*

Each year during the Patronal Festival of Winchester's glorious cathedral the bishop of the diocese publicly recalls the dean and chapter to their solemn accountability for the fabric, worship and ministry of the Foundation. Throughout Dean Stancliffe's seventeen years in office all knew that this trust would be impeccably discharged under his gentle wisdom and passionate artistry. That is the man who shines through his sermons, and all who read this selection will realize what a fortunate bishop I was to have him as a colleague, next-door neighbour and friend.

Sermons on the whole do not make very good reading. But Michael Stancliffe is a very private person with a genuine distrust of preaching. 'We do not mean to assert ourselves', he says. 'We do not consciously set ourselves over against them, still less do we intentionally set ourselves above them. But that is what it comes to.' So he is more at home in his library than in the pulpit. Distilled from quiet reading and rumination, these sermons sound more like vintage conversation or the exquisite essays he writes for 'The Daily Telegraph'. Dr Cleverley Ford, the first director of the College of Preachers in London, considers him one of the few great preachers of our day. Even so we have to thank the other members of the cathedral chapter for overcoming their dean's reluctance to publish.

Here is poetry rather than rhetoric. It happens that Dean Stancliffe first 'did' his theology and only later came to the poets. Theirs is the sphere in which, more and more, he finds his theological insight. He seems to wait until some changeless truth from the Bible becomes lit with the strangeness of an artist's vision, resonant with new associations. The same skill is often turned to humorous effect when an overworked phrase is put to serve some richer meaning — as of the Fall of mankind when Adam and Eve 'tumbled to it that they had lost something priceless'; or of Christ crucified, the still centre of the world 'while men made circles round him'.

Yes, Michael Stancliffe preaches like that householder who 'bringeth forth out of his treasure things new and old'. But this imposes on him the agonizing problem of 'our conflicting loyalties to the past and the future'. Precisely because for him that conflict will never be resolved, he is 'conservative' in the true sense, knowing how humanity needs the heritage which the Church exists to conserve. 'Our most urgent duty is not the further restructuring of the Church, the further contriving of its organic unity, the further up-dating of its liturgy or the further relaxing of its ethic — but defending the ancient springs, unstopping wells, cleaning streams, conserving conduits.' Yet what could be more unconventional than a Christian sermon entirely devoted to the legend of the Green Knight, or an Easter homily on a painting in Istanbul? This is a prophet indeed — remembering what has been for the sake of what shall be.

John V. Taylor
Bishop of Winchester 1975—85

1

Looking Into Things [1]

*

Because the bath was nearly full some of the water slopped over when Archimedes stepped into it. Many people would have seen no more than a mess on the bathroom floor — and that is all the camera would have seen. But Archimedes saw more than that, saw deeper than that. He saw a law of physics of universal significance, a principle which is still true centuries after the mess has been mopped up.

Again, most of the influential inhabitants of Jerusalem in 701 BC saw a mess of another kind — the surrounding countryside devastated and their city itself besieged by the armies of Assyria. But because they were not men of vision they could not see why this should be so. Were they not God's people, and a very devout people, continually thronging the Temple, observing all the sabbaths and other appointed feasts, and punctiliously offering endless sacrifices? However, there was one man of vision among them, the prophet Isaiah. He saw all that the others saw — the enemy camps outside the walls and the full churches, so to call them, inside. But he also saw something else inside — proud self-sufficiency, bribery, corruption, graft, the oppression of the weak and the denial of justice to the poor. Further, because he was a man of vision, Isaiah saw a connection between all those things. Like Archimedes he saw a principle of universal significance in that mess in and around Jerusalem, a principle which is still true, namely, that when religion is only a matter of outward form and the moral law of Almighty God is denied or flouted, then

[1] November 1970

1

things go ill. 'Where there is no vision, the people perish' (Proverbs 29.18).

Yet again, all that many saw in the house of Simon the leper at Bethany was a woman emptying a pot of extremely expensive ointment over a faith-healer from Galilee. It was an outrageous waste. The ointment might have been sold and the considerable proceeds given for the relief of human distress. But the two persons chiefly concerned saw very much more than that. She saw in him something very much more than a faith-healer from the provinces, just as he saw in her something very much more than an extravagant exhibitionist — and what they saw in each other is valued to this day.

There is much more in most things — and in most persons — than lies upon the surface or appears at first sight. We have considered just three examples, and further instances could be multiplied. Just think what Coleridge saw in the shooting of an albatross and what Blake saw in a grain of sand; what Botticelli saw in the legend of the birth of Venus and Handel saw in a verse of the book of Job; what Moses saw in a burning bush and what the author of the Book of Revelation saw in all manner of things. Above all, think what Jesus saw in, for instance, mustard-seed and wineskins, in a hold-up on the Jerusalem-Jericho road and in bridesmaids late for a wedding; in an unjust steward and in a good shepherd. In the Poets' Corner in the south transept of Westminster Abbey there stands the late Sir Jacob Epstein's bronze bust of William Blake — and if you go and look at Blake, you will find that he looks at you; more than that, he looks *into* you. Even more so did Jesus of Nazareth look at men and into men, so that he could see what others did not see, and know what others did not know, even about themselves. Being a person of vision he could see that Peter would deny him, that Judas would betray him, and that he himself would be put to death.

He saw this last with peculiar clarity, for it is commonly the fate of the man of vision and insight to be without honour in his own country and in his own day. The majority of those around him — his shallow-sighted neighbours, his literal-minded contemporaries — these have little use for the man of vision, the artist, the poet, the prophet, the mystic. Unable to see as far as he does, they feel uncomfortable, they don't understand, they dismiss his vision as illusion and, injured in their pride, mock and satirize him and decry him as a fraud. Later, when they discover that he has seen through them, has seen in their hearts what they hoped was well-hidden, then they secretly fear him; they attempt to silence him, sometimes to destroy him. He who sees too far, and therefore knows too much, is best removed: 'Let him be crucified.'

But, 'Where there is no vision the people perish.' Those who despise or reject the imaginative insights of the artist, poet, prophet, or mystic, those who imagine that virtually the whole of truth lies on the surface and so fail to see things as they really are — such people are heading for disaster. Shallow sight has accounted for the collapse of many empires, as it has accounted for the break up of many individual human beings. A classic example is given in the opening chapters of the First Book of Samuel. The chief priest Eli was old, and his eyes had waxed dim; his sons, the young priests Hophni and Phinehas, were living on the fat of the sacrifices in vice and great luxury; men of vision there were none, and the people were simply in the dark. As the Bible puts it: 'The word of the Lord was precious in those days; there was no open vision.' In such circumstances no one could see things as they really were. And then the Philistines came. In the opening battle the Israelite vanguard was routed, and in their blindness the people hurriedly fetched the Ark and rushed with this fetish into battle, shouting a great shout so that the earth rang again. The Philistines guessed what that shout meant, redoubled their efforts, captured the Ark, and easily overran the country. A secret weapon and a lot of patriotic shouting cannot save a people who have not been taught to look beyond the ends of their noses, or to recognize the existence of such invisible qualities as truth, integrity and righteousness. It was because there was a man of vision, Isaiah, in Jerusalem in 701 BC, and because the people on that occasion gave heed to his message that the siege was withstood and the enemy forced to withdraw. But where there is no vision the people perish.

And for three reasons: first, if we have no vision, and all the truth we recognize is what lies on the surface, then we shall perhaps be successful materialists, and we shall survive as long as we do not come up against someone with more brute strength, slick wits and animal cunning than ourselves. But if we have no vision we remain ignorant of all but a fraction of the truth, ignorant of most things as they really are, ignorant of all that the camera cannot see; ignorant, therefore, amongst other things, of God himself. And that, in the end, means that we perish.

But secondly, if we have no vision, such truth as we can see we see distorted and out of focus, out of proportion. We treat what is but a part as the whole, what is relative as absolute. So shallow sight means also a literal mind, and we rush an ark into battle, or an isolated text into debate, fondly but falsely imagining that we have the invincible power of truth on our side. And that in the end also means defeat.

And thirdly, if we have only shallow sight we shall have only a hard heart, for a narrow mind means a narrow sympathy. The scribes and Pharisees of Christ's day knew what they knew exceeding well. They had their scriptural texts by heart, and by them they ruled their own lives and the lives of others with an iron rigidity. They knew, they thought, exactly where they were and what was what — and accordingly crucified Jesus who didn't fit into their tidy little pattern. But what are those scribes and Pharisees now but monuments to the truth of Paul's words: 'The letter killeth; it is the spirit that giveth life'? Where there is no vision the people perish.

But who has this vision, this power of insight into things as they really are? Not all men certainly — or rather, some men have it to a markedly greater degree than others — the artist, the poet, the prophet, the mystic. A wise people honours such men and pays attention to them — even though it finds them hard to understand and their message often distasteful. But how do we know they are telling the truth? May they not be frauds? Yes, some of them may be — and there were false prophets in Old Testament times. But the false prophet can usually be detected by the bigness of his boasts and by the popularity of his promises. The genuine prophet, however, is a man of great humility, and is not ashamed to confess that he does not know everything. And the genuine prophet often has unpleasant things to say; he says what he has seen to be the truth, and not what he thinks will please the majority. Only the false prophet will claim that all is easier than it seems, that all men are angels, that there is nothing on earth to be afraid of, and certainly nothing in heaven to be afraid of.

Honour the man of vision then, and pay serious attention to what he says. But also, strive to become persons of keen insight yourselves. We are not most of us great visionaries, we can't all be an Archimedes, an Isaiah, a Blake. At the same time most of us can learn to see more than a camera does. A camera, they say, is dead accurate; but as Day Lewis remarked, what is the use of accuracy if it is dead? Start by expecting to see in things and in persons more than meets the eye. Do not be dazzled by surface glitter nor dismayed by apparent dullness. Do not be led astray by catchy sounds on the one hand, nor by ugly sounds on the other. Do not be satisfied with clichés, and always beware of the sin of taking things too literally — the letter killeth; it is the spirit that giveth life. So seek the help and inspiration of the Holy Spirit, who spake by the prophets, and part of whose work it is to lead us into all truth. Have the patience and discrimination to look *into* things, not just at them. Above all, and again and again, look not at, but into, Jesus — into what he said, into what he did, into what he is.

As the coming season of Advent reminds us, this is ultimately a matter of life and death. For where there is no vision the people perish.

2

Beyond the Frame [1]

*

Being a little man, and right at the back of the crowd, Zacchaeus hadn't a hope of seeing Jesus go by in the procession. So he did the sensible thing and shinned up a tree. It meant taking his feet off the ground for a bit — but it gave him an excellent view, and he saw Jesus clearly. And Jesus, who always had his eyes about him, saw Zacchaeus, stopped to talk with him, and then and there invited himself to dinner with him. It was a great day for Zacchaeus.

The story might well end differently today. Zacchaeus would not now have to climb a tree. He could stay with his feet on the ground, having provided himself with a periscope. Better still, he could stay at home and see it all on television — always assuming that those who decide what we shall or shall not see should think it worthwhile training the camera on that little procession.

But Zacchaeus had neither periscope nor television — and for this obvious and fundamental reason among others: there was virtually no glass in the world in Christ's time. It was not until the fifteenth-sixteenth centuries that clear colourless glass became at all common. Then, and in consequence, men's lives and men's thinking were utterly transformed.

Many were the ways in which clear colourless glass now gave men a new outlook. From within his own home a man could now look out of windows which were no longer 'the wind's eyes', could look out on the world at any time, at any

[1] October 1970

season, without getting wet or cold. A man could now have spectacles to aid his failing or faulty eyesight, and so add ten to twenty years to his working life. He could peer through a telescope, and so extend his sight to great distances, while the microscope gave him a window into a new world beneath his nose. Above all there was the looking-glass, a window enabling a man to see and so consider himself far, far more clearly than had ever been possible with a plate of polished metal or the surface of a bucket of water.

Of all our physical senses the sense of sight is the most significant and compelling. In the long run it is what we see, and the way in which we see, that conditions most of our thinking and behaving. Seeing is believing. And the keener sight which the invention of clear glass has given us has most powerfully affected the whole of our outlook — intellectually and spiritually as well as physically. We know and understand ourselves and our world enormously better because of the telescope and the microscope, the looking-glass and so on, and it is not without significance that Spinoza, the philosopher who had so much to do with shaping the way we now think, began his working life as a grinder of lenses. But while man's outlook has sharpened it has at the same time narrowed. The depth and distance of his vision have been extended, but his field of vision has contracted. He knows himself better, but his concern for his neighbour is less; and his concern for God is less still. It is much easier than it was to look to his own things; it is harder to look also to the things of others.

And for this reason: what you see through a pair of spectacles or a microscope, in a looking-glass or on a TV screen, is a *picture in a frame.* Your attention is focused on a sharply defined but strictly limited field. Within that field you see things far more clearly than you would otherwise see them, and you see much that would otherwise be invisible to you. But what you see you see in isolation, cut off from the whole of which it is part. To that part all your attention is drawn and given; the rest you do not see with the same concern — if indeed you see it at all. What the looking-glass, newspaper photograph or TV screen shows is framed. And to that extent it is a distortion of the truth. For the whole truth about anything can only be known if it is seen in its total setting, in its relation to the whole of which it is a part. Moreover since man is primarily interested in himself, so he tends in any case to look at what most immediately concerns him — his pride, his power and his pocket — and when he looks at his pride, his power and his pocket in the way he's learned to look at things in the last four centuries — with a narrowly focused attention on what is in the frame and with small concern for the whole which lies beyond the frame — then he inevitably has a still greater concern for himself and a still smaller concern for his neighbour; and God may well be excluded from his ken altogether.

Now this may seem far-fetched, but the fact remains that in the very centuries when the power of the human eye has been so greatly increased — that eye through which the greatest impressions are made on our minds — in those very centuries there has been an increasing concern with parts rather than with wholes, with analysis rather than with synthesis, with the self rather than with the other, with atoms rather than with God. Europe, Asia and Africa have been split into highly competitive nations; the Western Church has been divided into many churches; society has been broken into self-conscious classes and unions; and all the while man has become more and more concerned with his own self and with his own rights as an individual. Except where the Christian tradition has been vigorously upheld by a Wilberforce or Shaftesbury, civilized man has in fact in the last four centuries treated his fellow-men more callously than in the preceding thousand years — and certainly treated himself more carefully. When your feet are firmly on the ground and you are peering through a glass eyepiece you are in fact wearing blinkers. You only see what is straight in front of you; you don't have much concern for what is in the shadows on either side. You don't notice the wounded man lying in the gutter beside the Jerusalem-Jericho road. You don't spot the little man up in the tree at the back of the crowd.

This was not the way of Jesus. His depth of vision went far indeed. He could see in Peter, for instance, latent qualities which would make him the ideal man on whom to build the Church. But neither the keenness of Christ's insight nor the length of his foresight were allowed to narrow the width of his field of vision. He did not specialize; he had an eye for everyone; he always had his eyes about him; not even his enemies were beyond his loving concern.

Therefore: 'Look not each of you to his own things but each of you also to the things of others' (Philippians 2.4). Yes, we have known that from our childhood days — and by the grace of God we are not completely selfish, but do in some measure peer into some things as well as looking-glasses. But we should have a wider charity and concern if we always remembered that frames, by their very nature, have their limitations. Whatever be the frame — a scientific law, a religious dogma, a political manifesto, a colour bar, a national frontier, an intellectual fashion, even an examination syllabus — whatever the frame the Christian will always look beyond its edges. By all means let us get hot under our collars about the colour bar — we ought to; but if at the same time we don't get hot under the collar with ourselves every time we treat *any other person whatsoever* as outside our interest, beneath our contempt or beyond the pale of our charity and our sympathy, then we are simply being hypocrites.

Look not each of you to his own things, but each of you also to the things of others. And we might all do a great deal worse than follow the example of Zacchaeus more often than we do by taking our feet off the ground for a bit and climbing up to where we can see more clearly, to where we can see Jesus. Oddly enough, the best way to do that is to kneel down and shut our eyes.

3

The Still Centre [1]

*

Consider a revolving wheel — the outer rim linked by spokes to the axle at the hub. The wheel is turned by power coming from the centre and the spokes convey that power to the rim. We know that a mark, say, halfway down a spoke moves round slower than a mark out on the rim — it describes a much smaller circle in precisely the same time. The nearer the mark is to the wheel's centre, the slower it will revolve; and it is, I believe, true to say that at the very centre where the spokes meet and whence the driving force comes, at the very centre of the revolving wheel, there is theoretically a point which is utterly and completely still.

Or — and I take the image from Charles Williams' novel *The Greater Trumps* — consider a busy road junction where four or five important streets meet and the traffic lights have broken down. There is a constant movement of vehicles of all kinds from and to all directions, and a constant roar of engines. Yet there is no confusion because, in the very centre of the circling traffic, there stands a helmeted, white-cuffed figure. He is silent, still, rooted to that central spot; yet he controls all and imposes order upon all. There is nothing stiff or death-like about his stillness; from time to time his arms and hands move deliberately and imperiously, and his body turns decisively within two or three square feet. But in contrast to all the noise and movement that is going on around him, the policeman on point duty is silent and still.

[1] February 1970

So also — and the idea will be familiar to readers of *Burnt Norton* — in the midmost point of the whole creation, at the still centre, God is — as he was in the beginning and ever shall be. Around him all is motion, sound, change, decay — galaxies circling, seasons and years and centuries circling, tides ebbing and flowing, sap rising and leaves falling, blood going round and round in the bodies of lions and men and mice. At the still centre, controlling all, moving all, Lord of all power and might, God is. With him there is no variableness, neither shadow of turning; he is the same yesterday, today and for ever.

Less regular and orderly than the movements of heavenly bodies and earthy bloodstreams are the gyrations of sinful men, men who in our less giddy moments are conscious of him who is Alpha and Omega, our maker and our judge and in whom we live and move and have our being. One such man was Elijah, who was caught up in the whirl of Israelite power-politics in the ninth century BC. One day he stood on Mount Carmel, supreme and alone as the one prophet of God; the day after he was down in the valley and flying for his life from the wrath of Jezebel. His high and exultant faith had melted away, and reaching the desert he laid himself down under a juniper bush and desired to die. In the stillness of the night in the desert new strength came to him, and on he went, on deeper into the desert, until he came to Horeb, the mount of God. And there he found faith and courage again, found them in the Lord. And where did he find the Lord? Not, we are told, in the roaring of the wind, nor in the commotion and convulsion of the earthquake, nor in the terrible power of the fire — but in a still small voice. He had reached the still point at the centre.

Eight centuries later God himself came down from heaven and through taking flesh entered the revolving stream of change and decay and lived in the midst of giddy twisting men. And one of his most telling characteristics was his stillness. In Jesus, busy and giddy and demented humans found peace and repose. 'Come unto me, all that travail and are heavy laden, and I will refresh you', he invited them. So Mary came and sat at his feet and was still, and busy Martha was urged to do likewise. Lunatics were found sitting at his feet, composed and in their right minds. And the words that he spoke were neither clever chat nor idle gossip, neither vulgar boasting nor loud opinion; such words as he spoke were recognized as words of love, of truth, and of no ordinary power and authority. Experienced boatmen panicked around him, but Jesus had merely to say to the elements, 'Peace, be still', and there was a great calm. Even when the wildest cyclone of human sin and demonic evil broke upon him, his stillness remained. Cross-examined by men bent upon his destruction, he held his peace — he *held* his peace. Nailed to the cross he remained unmoved while men made circles round him and taunted him to prove his divinity by coming down from the cross. Being the person he was, he stayed where he was — at the still centre; and, as many of those who have not called themselves Christians have recognized since, he mastered that scene on the green hill and was not mastered by it.

For the still centre is the source of all life and power and might. At the still centre of the cross, immense power was generated, radiating a pardon and peace that we know yet; and from the still centre of the tomb resurrection came. Judas, so dizzy with his twistings that he could not keep still, went and hanged himself. But those others who had been closest to Jesus, after the first panic, came together again and with much fear if not with much faith, with much love if not with much hope, waited, kept still and so witnessed the risen Lord and were filled with his power.

'Be still and know that I am God' (Psalm 46.10): so we are commanded, as the winds and waves of the Sea of Galilee were commanded. We are to be still because, by that means, we may come closest to God, to the core and centre of all things. We are to be still because, by that means, we may sit at his feet, clothed and in our right minds and able to hear the still, small voice. We are to be still because, by that means, we may be delivered from dizziness and business and may find both the peace that passes understanding and the source of all power and might. Be still and know that I am God.

But it is important to be clear about what that command means and what it does not mean. In the first place it means that we must be silent — not completely and perpetually of course, though there are some in every generation whom God calls into complete silence. But the majority of us are called to serve and know God in the world and not apart from it; and it is demanded of us that we should be much more silent than we generally are, that we should be quicker to hear and slower to speak. It is instructive that Christ's command to the storming wind and waves, 'Be still', is literally, in the Greek, 'Be muzzled' or 'Be gagged'. So many have so much to say so loudly today, that we cannot easily hear a still small voice through the pandemonium which masquerades as free speech. In such circumstances it is a high duty for Christians to set an example of patience, restraint and control of their own free speech, to think before they utter and to pray before they think.

In the second place the command, 'Be still', means that we are, as far as our creaturely state allows, to be motionless from time to time; to go into desert places and rest a while; to use periodically such abstinence that, our flesh being subdued to the spirit, we may obey the godly motions that radiate from the still centre; and not only in Lent but at all times the command, 'Be still', means we are to strive to be unbusy, unanxious, unhurried. We are to consider the lilies of the field and not be over-anxious about the morrow. We are to choose with Mary the better part and sit down at the feet of God and not always be cumbered with much serving. Still more are we to be at pains not to become busy little revolutionaries for ever coming and going and plotting and scheming and twisting and turning. Remember Judas Iscariot.

And thirdly, the command, 'Be still', does not mean that we are to be inactive and doing nothing, sleepy as dormice, stagnant as scummy ponds. On the contrary, the stillness of God is a stillness that is vibrant with energy, the stillness that is the source of all power and might and life; as the still point at the axle-centre drives the wheel, as the policeman on point-duty controls the traffic. So much human activity is worthless and ineffective today simply because the actors lack authority and power and control; and they lack authority and power and control because they are not still at the centre, but fritter away their energies in ungodly motions doing nothing significant — like the batteries of a car that has been put away with its lamps left on, lamps which blaze away all night illuminating nothing but the inside of the garage doors. Therefore we are commanded not just to be still but, 'Be still, and know that I am God'. Be still, and in the stillness of true prayer (not in the chatter which often passes for prayer) know that God *is* and that he is Lord of all power and might. Then, having come into the centre and been still and known God, we find ourselves full of power and might — and out we must go, for the divine energy won't have it otherwise — out we must go that in our several ways we may bring others back into the stillness to know the greatest of all secrets, to know God. He will not be known in sound and fury, as Elijah discovered; pandemonium is the noise of all devils. But God is known in the still small voice, and to hear that voice and to reach that still centre we have to learn to be very still ourselves.

4

A Time to Keep Silence[1]

*

'Yes; Geoffrey Day is a clever man if ever there was one. Never says anything: not he.' The speaker is one of Thomas Hardy's west country characters in *Under the Greenwood Tree.*

'Geoffrey Day is a clever man if ever there was one. Never says anything; not he.'

'Never', agrees another.

'You might live wi' that man, my sonnies, a hundred years, and never know there was anything in him.'

'Ay; one o' these up-country London ink-bottle chaps would call Geoffrey a fool.'

'Ye never find out what's in that man: never', said Spinks. 'Close? ah, he is close! He can hold his tongue well. That man's dumbness is wonderful to listen to.'

'There's so much sense in it. Every moment of it is brimmen over wi' sound understanding.'

That's how my text of *Under the Greenwood Tree* runs. But there seems to be a variant reading which, while not altering the sense, states it more strikingly:

'Silent? ah, he is silent! He can keep silence well. That man's silence is wonderful to listen to.'

'There's so much sense in it. Every moment of it is brimmen over with sound understanding.'

Not all silence is so full and deep and sensitive. Not all

[1]   August 1979

silence is golden. There is the leaden silence of a vacuum, the dead silence of a tomb, the empty silence of an uninhabited desert. There is a silence which is the carapace of the shy, the virtue of fools, the refuge of cowards, the shell of the lazy, the castle of the self-sufficient egoist. But in the main, silence is divine, it is golden; it is full and deep and sensitive, almost alive and certainly powerful. And we shall the better estimate its quality and power by reflecting upon the disintegration and destruction which so often follow upon its absence. For sound, the breaking of silence, can (and often does) break much else besides. Trumpets and shouts destroyed Jericho; a musical note of a particular frequency will shiver a goblet to splinters; aircraft breaking the sound-barrier can smash an acre of glasshouses. If we happen to live and try to sleep within a mile or two of a major airport we do not need to be reminded of the destructive power of sound; and, for all of us, the sudden squeal of the brakes of a car or the rasping screech of a mechanical saw can shiver our spines; while the various drills which bore into our roadways and our teeth seem to threaten to pierce and split our brains, to disintegrate our very beings. How much the sheer noise of twentieth-century life is contributing to the increasing destruction of our mental health I do not know — but pandemonium is totally devilish. It is the very opposite of silence; it is the din of hell.

Nor are our machines the worst offenders. It is the sounds made by our own mouths which do most damage to individual men and to communities of men. Recall what brought to an end the association of those who were building the Tower of Babel. Recall the sounds which persuaded Pilate to order the crucifixion of Jesus. Recall the voice of Hitler and the destruction which *that* did.

Nor does a man have to be a Hitler for his words to be destructive of human relationships. Obvious enough is the hurt done by gossips and backbiters, by controversialists with a gift for spite, critics with a taste for cruelty. But equally damaging to human relationships and human society can be the monotonous rumbling of bores, the chatter of birdwits, the grumbling of the discontented, the bragging of the boasters, the silky speech of the seducers and, by no means least, the preaching of the improvers.

The preaching of the improvers — and that means (or should mean) most of us, Christians and Humanists, clergy and laity alike, reformers of every kind. We all wish — or ought to wish — to help others to become happier and healthier and finer than they are; and as Christians we believe that, with God's help, we have the power to do so and the duty to do so. We have a 'mission' to them, as we know — and it is part of that mission to go into all the world and preach the gospel to every creature. We wish for them to have what we have been given, and to become as fortunate as we are. And so we address ourselves to them; we break silence and speak to them. We argue with them as honestly as we can; we try to prove, in all sincerity, that some of their beliefs are untrue or their practices wrong; we try to demonstrate, in all humility, why we think *our* beliefs are true and *our* practices right; and we seek to persuade them to give up being what they are that they may become like us and share our good fortune. We do not mean to assert ourselves. We do not consciously set ourselves over against them, still less do we intentionally set ourselves above them. But that is what it comes to. That is what it often looks like to them. And (is it not so?) again and again the result is the opposite of what we hoped for, and our speech is destructive of understanding between us. For those we thus address feel that they are being talked at, got at, indoctrinated; their resistance is aroused, their defences go up. They resent what appears to them as our arrogance; they resent our assertiveness which appears to them as an interference with their human integrity. They resent, too, the fact that, while we expect them to take us seriously and to listen to us, we do not always appear to take them so seriously or to be really prepared to listen to them.

And that is where we go wrong. We speak so much in our desire that they may be happier and finer and that they may share what we so richly enjoy. But we do not allow a place for silence, we do not know the strength of silence and we have no faith in the power of silence. We do not understand that, as George Meredith put it, 'speech is the small change of silence'. We often teach and preach about the teaching and preaching of Jesus and are adept at spinning out ten plain words of his into two thousand of our own. But we do not sufficiently often think upon the silences of Jesus — his thirty years of silence before he ever began to preach; his silence in wilderness and on mountainside; in particular his silence before his accusers and how he held his peace when he hung upon the cross while the noisy revolutionaries, as is the way of revolutionaries, made rings round him and yelled their heads off at him. We wish to be, in the best and fullest sense of the word, the friends of those whom we long to save and 'convert' — but we have not grasped what is the greatest office of a friend: to lay down our lives for them, to put ourselves on one side for their sake.

Now I am not saying that there is no place for preaching — I should hardly be here if I believed that. I'm not saying we should not each of us speak to persuade others to accept what we honestly believe to be the truth. What I am saying is that before the speaking there must be silence, and that what we say, and how we say it, will come out of what we have learned in the silence about God, about ourselves, and about those whom we are trying to help. It is the silence — maybe short, maybe long, maybe half a minute, maybe half an hour, maybe half a lifetime — it is the silence that will create the conditions and the opportunity for us to speak, as it is in the silence that we shall be shown what we ought to say and how to say it.

We cannot too often reflect upon the creative power of silence, and we cannot too strongly emphasize the importance of our possessing ourselves in humility and patience to let the silence work. 'We know' (it has been said) 'that serious things have to be done in silence, because we do not have words to measure the immeasurable. In silence men love, pray, listen, compose, paint, write, think, suffer. These experiences are all occasions of giving and receiving, of some encounter with forces that are inexhaustible and independent of us. These are as easily distinguishable from our routines and possessiveness as silence is distinct from noise.'

What does this silence of which I am speaking require of us? Two things at least:

First: it means bringing ourselves in silence into the presence of God, jabbering much less to him, listening much more. It means becoming more sensitive to him, more open to him and to his inspiration. In this way, in such silence, we come to know him better — and, in consequence, to know ourselves better by contrast, to recognize more clearly our limitations, our own need of help and that we ourselves are very far from being perfect.

Secondly: being silent, cultivating that kind of silence which Geoffrey Day had, that silence which was so wonderful to listen to and which was brimming over with understanding — such silence involves a deliberate refusal to assert ourselves and to get at others; it involves putting ourselves alongside them, and as far as possible into their hearts and minds; coming to understand, as fully and as truthfully as we can, how the world looks to them, how we look to them, how God looks to them; why they believe as they do and behave as they do; it involves recognizing that they are human as we are human, that they too are made in the image of God, that in them too is something of the divine, something of the light that lighteth every man coming into the world. It involves so learning to respect them that we give up all thought of possessing them, of manipulating them, of indoctrinating them, of persuading them to cease to be themselves and to become facsimiles of ourselves. It involves holding ourselves in silent readiness to speak only when the time comes. The time will come, when, because they have learnt to trust us and respect us and recognize how much we care about them, they ask us to break silence, to speak, to tell them the secret of our patience with them and of our compassion for them. Certainly we have a mission to mankind. But it should always start from silence, and it should never become noisy. 'Be swift to hear, slow to speak' (James 1.19). 'For everything there is a season, and a time for every matter under the sun — a time to keep silence, and a time to speak' (Ecclesiastes 3.1, 7).

5

Stir Up

A Sermon before Advent [1]

*

See with the eyes of that part of your spirit which appreciates a work of art, together with the eyes of that part of you which should be aware of your cultural roots, a sheet of vellum on which an inscription has just been written. The ink is still wet, but the light of this winter afternoon is already fading and the work must stop. And anyhow a bell is ringing and the monk must leave the scriptorium and take himself off to chapel for Nones — leaving us the opportunity to study what he's been up to. The sheet on the desk is part of a book being made for the altar of the great Palatine Church just built for Charlemagne at Aachen at the turn of the eighth-ninth centuries.

Familiar as we are with newsprint and typescript we can't read fast enough; there's nothing in the characters themselves of newsprint and typescript to arrest our eye. But the text before us now is of a very different quality. Every character has character — as have all things that are hand-made — and not least the large decorative E with which the inscription begins. After that capital E an X, C, I, T — which suggest 'excitement' is to come. But this first word ends abruptly with an A, for this is Latin in front of us; and if my mistakes may be forgiven by those who are expert in the Carolingian pronunciation of Latin, the whole text runs as follows:

[1] November 1976

Excita, quaesumus domine, tuorum fidelium voluntates: ut divini operis fructum propensius exequentes, pietatis tuae remedia maiora percipiant. Per dominum.

It stops there. The priests would know the usual formula with which to end the prayer, and in any case the light was going and the bell was ringing.

The translation you know; you heard it some minutes ago:

Stir up, we beseech thee, O Lord, the wills of thy faithful people: that they, plenteously bringing forth the fruit of good works, may of thee be plenteously rewarded.

There is a considerable puzzle there — but leave that for the moment. It is with the stirring start that we must first concern ourselves. *Stir up, we beseech thee* — still the annual signal to good Anglican housewives to put the ingredients of the Christmas pudding into a bowl and to call every member of the household to come and lend a hand with the stirring. But it is not of pudding but of ourselves that the collect speaks; it is we who are to be stirred, and God who is asked to do the stirring. So we had best keep mum if we are satisfied with things as they are, with ourselves as we are. It is *we* who are to be stirred — and God who is prayed, almost commanded, to do the stirring. That is one of the arresting features of this collect; in most prayers God's name comes first — 'Our Father' or 'Almighty God', but this starts with two imperative monosyllables in English, *Stir up* — in Latin, *Excita* — literally, make to move and agitate an inert and stodgy mass, our *wills*. Our bodies are lazy enough when it comes to doing the things we ought to be doing; our intellects and imaginations can go quietly through a week without being unduly exercised about anything apart from what concerns our material well-being. But the will is the laziest of all our members — and not least at this time of year. All is on the ebb. It is the fall. Summer's heat has drained away and all its petals dropped. Autumn is sinking deeper into winter, the year is waning, life fading. Everything is running down. The clouds return after the rain, the doors are shut in the streets, desire fails, man goeth to his long home and the mourners go about the streets. Or ever the silver cord be loosed, or the golden bowl be *broken,* or the pitcher be *broken* at the fountain, or the wheel *broken* at the cistern. Then shall the dust return to the earth as it was. At such a season, in such a mood, the will is weakest, our self-starter most unreliable and prone to fail. Therefore: *Stir up, O Lord, the wills of thy faithful people.*

Of thy faithful people — not of mankind at large. No doubt the wills of all men need stirring, and we could all make a list of individual infidels whose wills we should be glad to see stirred into action. Maybe — but what we ask in this prayer is that the Church should be shaken up and ourselves stirred. It is easy to feel established and comfortably settled if we come regularly to church, say our prayers, and help lame dogs over stiles on the rare occasions when we come to a stile and happen to meet there a dog — and the dog lame. But Christians are called to do a lot more than that!

So much for the stirring start to this collect. Now the puzzle. Our perplexity is this: the reason given for praying that our wills be stirred up is so that, plenteously bringing forth the fruit of good works, we may of God be plenteously rewarded. Are you content that your Christian living should be inspired by that profit motive? Are you happy to accept the suggestion that the overriding purpose of your life should be this: to be so prolific in your good works to God and man that you may earn a bumper crop of advantages for yourself?

It is true that Jesus plainly spoke of rewards for those who follow him faithfully. But he also made it clear that he who seeks to save his life shall lose it. Remembering that, remembering too that 'charity seeketh not her own', how can we deliberately pray that we may be stirred to live in such a way that we may be paid top prices for our crop of good works?

It is a fact that the Latin collect with which we began,

which had been used throughout Western Europe on the Sunday next before Advent every year since the time of Charlemagne, suffered enormous violence when it was translated into English by Cranmer and his liturgical commission for our Book of Common Prayer. What the motive was cannot be known with any certainty. What is certain is that when Cranmer englished this collect he translated the first half with strict accuracy, the second half with no accuracy at all. It is almost the kind of work for which a boy would be sent to his headmaster. Literally translated the original would run: 'Stir up, we beseech, O Lord, the wills of thy faithful people, that they, seeking more readily the fruit of the divine work, may come to possess the greater remedies of thy piety.'

Which makes a deal of a difference. We should be asking that we may be stirred up to *seek* fruits rather than grow them, fruits of *God's* producing, not of our own; fruits of his divine work, all the blessings he has made available to us through the life, death and resurrection of Jesus Christ. And we are to seek these blessings not that we may have plentiful rewards, but rather that we may be given great *remedies* — not prizes for our perfection, but pills and prescriptions for our imperfections.

And that puts an entirely different complexion upon things, and the aptness of this collect to our present condition becomes plain indeed. All things may not be running down so literally or so fast as the writer of Ecclesiastes felt, but they are drawing towards an end. The old year is passing and next Sunday a new year begins for Christians, with Advent reminding them not only to prepare to celebrate at Christmas Christ's first coming to save us, but also to prepare us for his second coming to judge us. Next Sunday we shall be told that it is high time to awake out of sleep, the night being far spent and the day at hand. This week the collect should begin to get us moving. Summer's petals are all dropped, the light of the winter afternoon is fast fading, and a bell is ringing. We must go to prayers.

6

God Rest You Merry, Gentlemen

A Sermon for Christmas Day [1]

*

> God rest you merry, gentlemen,
> Let nothing you dismay

—and, as a contribution both to your merriment and to the defeat of dismay, here is a story. It's not a short story, and those who already know and love it must forgive my ruthless and prosaic abbreviation of it. And if it seems to have not much to do with Bethlehem or with our own situation in the midwinter of 1982 — well, Christmas is traditionally a time for games and puzzles, and if you need a solution to this puzzle you will find it at the end. Are you sitting comfortably? Then I'll begin.

Once upon a time, (here in Winchester, some think) a King called Arthur and his court were celebrating Christmas with all its medieval richness — twelve days of merriment to defeat that deep depression induced by all the cold and dark of midwinter in Northern Europe. There was churchgoing, feasting, carols and dancing, exchange of presents, telling of stories, playing of games. And on New Year's Day, just as dinner was beginning, something happened which instantly hushed the whole merry company. There rode into the Great Hall a man on horseback, a man whose clothes, skin, hair, even his horse, were all bright green. In one hand he held a bunch of holly, in the other a whacking great axe. 'I've heard of

[1]   December 1982

25

your reputation for honour, courage, and courtesy', said the Green Man, 'and I offer you a Christmas game. Let's see how brave and good you are. Let one of you take this axe and cut off my head. There's only one rule in the game. It's this: the man with the courage to take up this challenge must meet me a year from now and allow me to do to him what he now does to me.'

'What foolery', said the King. 'Then you are afraid!' 'Not at all', replied the King somewhat nettled, and rose to accept the challenge. 'It's wrong for the King's life to be risked', said Sir Gawain, 'let me do it'. All agreed that it was proper he should take the King's place. The Green Man dismounted, gave Gawain the axe, bent his head, bared his neck, and said 'Strike'. Gawain struck — and the head went rolling over the floor and among the feet of the lords and ladies at table. The Green Man fetched his head, gathered it into his arms and, speaking through its mouth, said: 'Right. Now keep your word. Meet me in a year's time in the Green Chapel.' And with that he mounted, rode out of the Hall, and disappeared.

So much for a bald summary of the start of this strange story, that poem called *Sir Gawain and the Green Knight* — a poem which is, in its own way, as great a work of art and superb craftsmanship as this nave in which we are gathered. William of Wykeham was building this here at exactly the same time as an unknown man in N. W. England was constructing, in celebration of Christmas, the poem of which I am reminding you.

To resume its story: when the Green Man had left the Hall Arthur and his company resumed their merriment. They let nothing them dismay. And when the twelve days of Christmas were over life returned to normal and the seasons came and went until, in autumn at All Saints-tide, Gawain with growing foreboding said goodbye to his companions, and rode out alone in search of the Green Chapel where honour required him to be in two months' time. The journey was long and hard; it was a cold coming he had of it in the bleak midwinter of N. W.

England. And time was running short when, on Christmas Day, he chanced upon a fine castle and asked for lodging. He was most warmly welcomed and invited to join the Christmas house party in the castle. Gawain was merry and let nothing him dismay, for the lord of the castle said that the Green Chapel about which Gawain asked was only a couple of miles away. 'After your long hard journey you need rest', said the lord. 'I shall go out hunting each day, but you shall have breakfast in bed, and get up when you feel like it, and we'll have a game: I will make you a present of whatever I catch in the chase, and you make me a present of whatever you happen to gain during the day.' It is agreed.

Next morning the lord rides out to hunt the deer — and the chase is described. The poet then returns to Gawain having his lie-in and just waking up when, click, he is suddenly wide awake hearing somebody stealthily opening his bedroom door. He peeps through the curtain and sees coming towards him the beautiful wife of the lord of the castle. He feigns to be asleep, she slips through the curtain and sits on his bed, and he pretends to wake with a start. He greets her gallantly: 'Forgive me for sleeping so long. I'll quickly get up and get dressed and join you downstairs.' 'I've a better idea', she replies: 'everyone's out hunting, and I've locked the door. Let me get into bed with you.' At some length, but with the greatest courtesy, Gawain excuses himself — but allows the lovely lady to give him a kiss before she leaves him. That evening the lord of the castle gives him a haunch of venison, and Gawain gives him one kiss.

The next day follows a similar pattern. The lord hunts the boar, the lady again tries to seduce Gawain — but is resisted, then allowed to give him two kisses. In the evening he is presented with the boar's head, and he gives the lord two kisses.

So to the third day, New Year's Eve. Gawain has not slept well. He knows tomorrow he must play the game and meet that Green Man and his axe. It's his last day. The lord goes hunting the fox, and again the lovely lady comes to Gawain's bedroom, looking more desirable than ever in a smashing dress which sweeps to her ankles but the bodice of which leaves very little to the imagination. And Gawain, on this the last day of his life, still resolutely walks the tight-rope between bad faith to his host and discourtesy to a lady. Finally she gives up trying to seduce him, but adds in so many words, 'Darling, won't you give me something to remind me of you'. 'I've only come with little luggage — I've nothing worthy to give you.' 'Well, at least let me give you something', — and proffers her ring. 'Dear Lady, not having anything to give you, I can't allow you to give anything to me.' 'Well, let me just give you a trifle — my girdle,' and she slips it off her hips. He won't touch it. 'Oh, come on', she says; 'it's only a belt — tho' as a matter of fact it's rather a special one. Anyone wearing it can't be killed.' And Gawain wavers . . . and then gives way — and she gives him three kisses and leaves him. That evening when the lord comes home, Gawain gives him three kisses and is given the skin of the fox.

New Year's Day. Gawain goes out into the wilds and finds the Green Chapel, 'the most evil holy place I ever entered', he said — a ruined pile of stones, like an entrance to the underworld. The icy air is loud with one single sound — of an axe being sharpened. The Green Man comes to meet him, compliments him on keeping his faith, tells him to take off his helmet and prepare to be repaid for the blow he dared to strike a year ago. Gawain obeys, bows his head, and the axe is lifted, whirled round, then poised to fall — but is lowered. It is raised a second time, whirled, poised — and lowered again. It is raised the third time, whirled, poised — and comes crashing down — but misses, only nicking the skin of the neck. Gawain leaps aside, draws his sword, and says: 'That's it. You've had your turn, and I've kept my faith. I owe you no more, and now am ready to fight you.'

And the Green Man answers; 'Well said. You've proved yourself. Our Christmas game is over. Your honour and truthfulness have only failed once. You may not recognize me, but I am your host of these last days. We agreed to exchange our winnings each evening. My wife kissed you once, then twice — and you paid me those kisses with complete honour, which is why I didn't bring the axe down the first two times. But you failed in one particular on the third day: you gave me my wife's three kisses; you did not give me her girdle. That was deceitful of you — but your motive was wholly good, which is why I only nicked your neck. Your motive was good: you loved life more than death — and so God's creatures should.'

Gawain admits his fault, leaves the Green Man, returns to Arthur and his court, tells his story concealing nothing, and all are merry and applaud him for having added considerably to the renown and honour of the Round Table.

Well, that's the story, a very prosaic summary of a marvellous work of literature. But what's it got to do with Christmas? If we are puzzled it is perhaps because we've forgotten what Christmas is really about. We so easily allow all the familiar and dearly loved pictures of a crowded inn, crude stable, ox and ass, a lowly couple, rough shepherds, rich kings and a bright star in a sky full of angels — we allow all that to distract our attention from the child in the crib, who he is, and why he's come. Why has he come? When he grew up he answered that question precisely: 'I am come that men might have life and have it more abundantly.' (John 10.10).

Christians have too often forgotten that, and appeared more interested in denying life and its joys. But the medieval poem of which I've been speaking says 'Yes' to life. Merriment and joy, laughter and fun and games, are what God wants his children to have. It doesn't pretend there are no difficulties, no miseries, no suffering, no death — but it does say that these should be seen in proper perspective, kept in their place, and not permitted to get us down. So, God rest you merry, gentlemen.

But, but — we live in a bleak midwinter, in a world that is

desperately cold and dark. There hangs over us all the threat of something more powerfully deadly than any Green Man's axe. We must assuredly not belittle the threat of a nuclear cataclysm, nor blink the decision we are all going to have to make within the coming months. But let us not kill ourselves with fear.

In the *Church Times* a week ago Miss Monica Furlong concluded a series of articles on the nuclear arms debate with these words:

> If we don't love life and one another perhaps it matters very little what gets destroyed. In our determined struggle NOT to deny the danger . . . there has to be a corresponding lightness of heart, of laughter, of joy, to remind us that life is after all worth living. Nothing will take us more surely down the deadly paths of war than depression and despair.

I believe that is profoundly true. It is the truth that *Sir Gawain and the Green Knight* affirms and celebrates with such verve and humour and joyous confidence — and it has its root in this faith: that the Christ child born in Bethlehem came that we might have life and have it more abundantly. So —

God rest you merry, gentlemen,
Let nothing you dismay,
Remember Christ our Saviour
Was born on Christmas day,
To save us all from Satan's power
When we were gone astray:
O tidings of comfort and joy.

7

The Fall

A Sermon for Sexagesima [1]

*

Humble yourselves therefore under the mighty hand of
God, that he may exalt you in due time. (1 Peter 5.6)

I will come back to Peter later. I begin with a lady. Her name
was Eve, and there's a reason for that. But it might have been
Alice — and there would be a reason for that. At least,
alongside that story we heard in the first lesson listen to this
extract from another well-known story — admittedly a good
deal slighter but equally unforgettable, and not without value
and significance when it comes to trying to understand what
expulsion from the Garden of Eden meant:

She found herself falling down what seemed a very deep
well. Either the well was very deep, or she fell very slowly,
for she had plenty of time as she went down to look about
her, and to wonder what was going to happen next. First,
she tried to look down, but it was too dark to see anything;
then she looked at the sides, and there she saw maps and
pictures hung upon pegs. She took down a jar from one of
the shelves as she passed; it was labelled 'ORANGE
MARMALADE' but to her great disappointment it was
empty; she did not like to drop the jar, for fear of killing
someone underneath . . . Down, down, down. Would the fall
never come to an end? 'I wonder how many miles I've fallen

[1]   February 1976

by this time?' . . . Down, down, down. There was nothing else to do, so Alice soon began talking again. 'Dinah'll miss me very much tonight, I should think!' (Dinah was the cat). 'I hope they'll remember her saucer of milk at tea-time. Dinah, my dear! I wish you were down here with me! There are no mice in the air, I'm afraid, but you might catch a bat . . . Do cats eat bats? . . . do bats eat cats?' . . . when suddenly, thump! thump! down she came upon a heap of sticks and dry leaves, and the fall was over.

Alice was not a bit hurt, and she jumped up in a moment: she looked up, but it was all dark overhead; before her was a long passage and the White Rabbit was still in sight, hurrying down it . . . and when she'd gone down it and turned the corner she found herself in a long, low hall . . .

There were doors all round the hall, but they were all locked; and when Alice had been all the way down one side and up the other, trying every door, she walked sadly down the middle, wondering how she was ever to get out again.

Suddenly she came upon a little three-legged table, all made of solid glass: there was nothing on it but a tiny golden key . . . but alas! either the locks were too large, or the key was too small, but at any rate it would not open any of them. However, on the second time round, she came upon a low curtain she had not noticed before, and behind it was a little door about fifteen inches high: she tried the little golden key in the lock, and to her great delight it fitted!

Alice opened the door and found that it led into a small passage . . . and she knelt down and looked along the passage into the loveliest garden you ever saw. How she longed to get out of that dark hall, and wander about among those beds of bright flowers and those cool fountains — but she couldn't even get her head through the doorway; 'and even if my head *would* go through', thought poor Alice, 'it would be of very little use without my shoulders. Oh, how I wish I could shut up like a telescope! I think I could, if I only knew how to begin.'

Though without suffering much damage to herself Alice, like Humpty Dumpty, had a great *fall.* And it is usual for theologians to refer to what happened to Adam and Eve in the Garden of Eden as The Fall. In fact, though the word 'fall' is common in the Bible, it does *not* appear in Genesis 3 and nowhere in the Bible is it used of the happenings recorded in Genesis 3. The nearest to it is in Romans where Paul speaks of Adam's 'transgression' — literally in the Greek a sideways slip, a false step, a lapse. But when theologians speak of the Fall they refer not so much to the false step but to its consequence, not to the slip but to the drop that followed. In Genesis 3 that consequence is described as expulsion and permanent exclusion from Paradise. From enjoying innocent and carefree happiness within God's garden, Adam and Eve found themselves suffering pain and hard labour outside. They tumbled to it that they had lost something priceless, that they were in a hole, that there was no way of getting out of it. *That* was the Fall of Man.

The act of falling, and the consequences of falling, are generally disagreeable. Almost the only pleasant falls are falling asleep or falling in love. Falling is disagreeable because, unless we are miners or pot-holers, most of us don't choose to go down holes; unless we are parachutists, professional gymnasts or divers, we don't willingly fall. For the majority of us, to fall off a wall, out of a tree, down the stairs, down a mountain, is to be suddenly *out of control*; without any warning, without any time to prepare for it, we find ourselves at the mercy of other forces and no longer in command of our own existence or direction. We don't fall as far as Alice, so we don't have any chance to notice the maps and books and things on the shelves around us. In those sickening giddy split seconds we have no time to feel much, let alone analyse our sensations. But if we could analyse them I suspect they would prove to be sensations of anxiety — anxiety about what we are losing and leaving behind ('Dinah will miss me very much tonight'), and anxiety about what the future is going to be. And if we survive and are still alive and conscious when we get to the bottom, then there's the question: 'How am I going to get out of this? I can't get up again by myself.' Holes are easy to fall down, but notoriously difficult to get out of. Anyone can drive a car into a ditch; it needs a crane or tractor to get it out again. The whole business of the Fall has a nightmare quality about it, the kind of nightmare in which you find yourself in a dark passage full of doors, and they are all locked, and the one key you have won't fit. Through a chink there's a glimpse of unattainable happiness and freedom — a garden with beds of flowers and cool fountains. But you can't reach it. Paradise is lost. You can't even get your head through the hole — but what would be the use if you could? What's the use of getting through with your head — with that bit of you that's full of rational thought and good intentions — if the rest of you is stuck outside?

The truth about the principle of evolution, that human beings are descended from something like monkeys, as a factual statement about the genetic development of life on this planet, nearly all of us accept. The researches of natural scientists admit of no other conclusion.

But some go much further and hold that the fact of evolution proves that man is steadily and inevitably progressing upwards towards a superior state. Setbacks he may have, but they cannot alter the general direction and ascent of man from his lowly beginnings to something higher. But our experience of what twentieth-century man — man 'come of age', so it's said — can do and does do to his fellow men, and not only to them but also to life as a whole on this planet, makes most of us hesitate to accept so optimistic a dogma.

On the other hand there is the Old Testament teaching that man is a fallen creature, one who has come down from a higher state he once enjoyed, and that nothing but a superhuman initiative can lift him up out of the hole into which he has fallen.

Faced with those two opposed beliefs it is not altogether surprising that the majority find the former the more credible.

The Fall

Knowing what we now know about man's past, the ancient Hebrew story of the Fall is simply unbelievable, not to be taken seriously. It is not just that the doctrine of the inevitability of man's upward progress is more comfortable. The Bible story of the Fall is simply incredible. What justification is there for believing that man was ever in a paradisal state which at some prehistoric moment he lost? Can an intelligent person today allow his understanding of the nature of man to be determined by a piece of Hebrew writing purporting to describe a Fall of Man at some particular moment in the past?

If we argue like that we have not rightly understood Genesis 3. We should not think of that story as a picture of what happened at one particular time in the past, but as a picture of a *continuous* happening to every Adam and Eve, every man and woman. This may not be apparent when we are young, but the older we grow the more we realize that it is *we* who are falling — that we are failing, are not what we were before. We get further and further from the comparatively simple, innocent, carefree happiness we remember we once enjoyed. We experience a growing sense of shame as we become more and more aware of the nakedness of our souls, a growing sense of guilt as we become more aware of temptations we've fallen into, and of good things we've left undone and so lost. But it seems too late now to save ourselves, and we have a growing anxiety about what's going to be the end of it all — for ourselves, for mankind as a whole, and not least for our 'descendants'. It's a hole we're in, and there seems no way out — lots of doors, but such keys as we've got won't open them. We have vivid glimpses of what life might be, visions of the garden of Paradise — but there seems no way whatever of getting there. The door is much too small;

which is another way of saying,
WE ARE MUCH TOO BIG;
too big for our boots,
too big to go through the eye of a needle,
too big to go through the door into the Kingdom of heaven.

'Oh how I wish I could shut up like a telescope! I think I could, if I only knew how to begin.'

The way to begin is to pay attention to St Peter:

> Humble yourselves under the mighty hand of God, that he may exalt you in due time.

8

Christ the Maker

One of a series of Sermons in Lent on
The Office and Work of Jesus Christ [1]

*

> Jesus, aware that all had now come to its appointed end,
> said in fulfilment of Scripture, 'I thirst'. A jar stood there
> full of sour wine; so they soaked a sponge with the wine,
> fixed it on a javelin, and held it up to his lips. Having
> received the wine, he said, 'It is accomplished!' He bowed
> his head and gave up his spirit (John 19.28-30).

'He said "It is accomplished" '; in the Authorised Version, 'He
cried with a loud voice'. All four gospel writers mention that
loud cry just before the end. It is John who records what the
cry was: in Greek, *'Tetelestai';* in the Latin of the Vulgate,
'Consummatum est'; in the English of the Authorised Version,
'It is finished'; in the English of today, 'It is accomplished'. Not
'It's all up', or 'It's the end'; those in defeat do not advertise
their surrender at the tops of their voices. But 'It is
accomplished' — the triumphant proclamation of an aim
realized, a task fulfilled, something of great value achieved —
the achievement bringing with it that sense of release and
freedom and elation that properly accompanies the completion
of something that a man has well and truly made — be it the
ploughing of a straight furrow or the completion of a *Mass in
B Minor,* a thing made that is right and lovely, a finished work
of art.

[1]   February 1982

In the course of one of his own unfinished poems, *The Book of Balaam's Ass,* David Jones has a passage in which he sets down in a series of disarmingly simple sentences what it is that such a work of art — 'a finished beauty' he calls it — does to us and for us:

> . . . the finished beauty that wins enchantment, gathers worship, holds the minds of men, becomes a word to work powerfully, generates makers' marvels, is a star for us, breaks our contingent misery with the noise of its perfection, day by day wins exaltation for us. (*The Roman Quarry*)

And that may be said not only of the works of a Shakespeare, a Bach or a Picasso, but equally of any master craftsman such as the ploughman, the engraver, the smith and the potter whose concentrated skill and conscientious attention to the finish of their works were celebrated in that passage read as the first lesson (Ecclesiasticus 38.24-34). In a good Anglo-Saxon six-letter word they were all *wrights*, working craftsmen. Alas, the word has become virtually obsolete except in surnames — Cartwright and Wainwright, Wheelwright and Arkwright — though some still speak of shipwrights, and more of playwrights — and we're all still familiar with wrought iron. But it's over a thousand years since the word was applied to Jesus — the Lindisfarne Gospels translating Mark 6.3 — 'Is not this the wright, the son of Mary?' Which reminds us that he who cried from the cross 'It is accomplished' spent the greater part of his life as a village craftsman — a carpenter, a wright, a joiner as we should call him nowadays — that is, one whose art lay in joining, putting together, different bits of this and that to make something other, something other that would give service and delight to his neighbours.

That is to say, he who was doing something, making something, on the cross, so that there came a moment when he could exclaim, 'It is accomplished' — this person was one whose only apprenticeship had been served in making things and was therefore well versed in *what goes into the making of an artist.* Five things in particular:

First: having a vision of what might be, and using the imagination to see this and that becoming that other which the vision has put before him.

Secondly: exercising a most patient respect for the raw materials, learning all about them, the way they go, what they can do and what they can't do — and bending himself to them almost as much as he bends them to himself.

Thirdly: knowing his tools, loving and valuing them as parts of himself, exchanging this one for that as the work requires, and using them always with an exquisite precision and a most disciplined control.

Fourthly — and this point is often overlooked — recall that for most artists one of the most difficult problems is getting the right things in exactly the right place. I suspect that one of the persistent headaches — or is it heartaches? — of an artist is placing each object, and therefore each stroke of pencil or brush, in such a way that it is neither too big nor too small; neither too weighty nor too light; and that one of the truest ways to bring out the significance of an object is not to score the paper with a heavy line, not to use a more strident colour, but to surround the object in question with a space of no significance. I say 'space of no significance', for that is what it is to the casual observer. But of course it is nothing of the sort. That area of no apparent significance is of incalculable importance to the whole — as are empty spaces, free of clutter, in a building like this; as are the rests in a musical score; as are the silent spaces in our own lives. We all know the perils of voids, and what the Devil can do with the idle. But it is time we remembered how much has been contributed to the growth of man by the existence of the wilderness.

Fifthly: from start to finish, having the faith and the courage to begin, to carry on and to complete the work — whatever the cost in time, in concentration, in weariness, and whatever the cost in strength required to resist the temptation to lose hope and give up in despair, and the temptation to sell the soul and settle for the second-rate or some other form of insincerity. There is not one of us — for man is a maker by nature in a way no other animal is, and there is something of an artist in each one of us — there is not one of us who does not know something of what it costs to make something that is honest and true, lovely and of good report — be it an essay, a letter or a poem, the singing of an anthem or the rowing of a race, the creating of a painting or the baking of a loaf. In each case, *mutatis mutandis,* we undertake something the beginning of which can be really fearful; the carrying on of which is demanding, even exhausting; and the end of which we can only see in imagination. To quote David Jones again:

> Making a work is not thinking thoughts but accomplishing an actual journey. There are the same tediums; strugglings with awkward shapes that won't fit into the bag, the same mislayings, as of tickets, the missings of connections, the long waits, the misdirections, the packing of this that you don't need and the forgetting of that which you do, and all such botherations, not to speak of more serious mishaps (*The Anathemata*, Preface).

These, surely, were at any rate some of the lessons learned amidst the sawdust and shavings of the joiner's shop and artist's studio in Nazareth: the primacy and authority of vision and the need to exercise imagination; immense respect for the raw materials; the loving care and disciplined use of tools; the importance of silent spaces; and the realization that the making of anything worthwhile — that which is true, honest, pure, lovely and of good report — is not thinking thoughts but accomplishing an actual journey which does not end until the work is accomplished and the artist can say: 'It is finished.'

So the Christ's journey started literally enough with a going out to John at a riverside, on through a wilderness, thence round and about in Galilee and Judaea, and finally up, up, up — up to Jerusalem, up to an Upper Room, up to the top of a hill, up onto the cross. Throughout the journey he kept before him the vision of what was to be made and the imagination to see *how* it was to be made. His tools were his hands, his words, his prayers. And his raw materials — very raw in the majority of cases — were the things and the persons encountered on the way. These he treated with infinite patience and respect, making the best of the best in each *and* making the best of the *worst* in each — accepting all their miscellaneous variety, their knottiness, their flaws, their unamenableness, their hardness, with no surrender of his own integrity or faith or hope or love — and making of all this, through his art and craftsmanship and use of silent spaces, nothing less than the salvation of the world and the beginnings of the New Creation.

This was the thing wrought by the son of Mary, the work of art finally accomplished on the cross:

> the finished beauty that
> wins enchantment,
> gathers worship,
> holds the minds of men,
> becomes a word to work powerfully,
> generates makers' marvels,
> is a star for us,
> breaks our contingent misery with the
> noise of its perfection,
> and day by day wins exaltation for us.

9

Come On and Get Up

A Sermon for Easter Day [1]

*

My sermon this morning is a painting — the most moving painting I've ever seen. No description in words can begin to express all that it is and says. But it is with poor inky words that we must make do, and I can only pray that they will show you something, give you something, and perhaps send you to look for the painting itself.

But first: its frame, its setting. It is on a ceiling two thousand miles from here. Away to the east, where daily there is resurrection — the rising of the sun — and on the very brink of Europe, lies the fabulous city of Byzantium, Constantinople, Istanbul — that city beside the Golden Horn, a city ringed with ancient walls and crossed by the ruins of ancient aqueducts, a city of wharves and markets, palaces and hovels, mosques, minarets and domes; the capital of Christendom for over a thousand years until its capture by the Turks when Henry VI was king of England and William Waynflete Bishop of Winchester. And on the hill at the heart of the city stands a gigantic tomb: once the great cathedral church of the Holy Wisdom, then a mosque, and now a museum — a vast space of stupendous architectural engineering but almost wholly bare, without glory, empty of virtually all decoration and furnishing, and containing not a cubic centimetre of holiness. It left me cold — as I have since read it left Osbert Lancaster cold:

[1] April 1983

Almost the first act of the conqueror in 1453 was to turn the great church into a mosque, which was a disaster; almost exactly five hundred years later Kemal Ataturk converted it into a museum, which was a greater disaster. The slight change of function involved in the former metamorphosis, although unfortunate, was not lethal, but the complete suspension of function imposed by its present status is the kiss of death; it is far better for the House of God to fall into the hands of the infidel than to pass into the custody of the Office of Works. No great building in the world is so completely lacking in atmosphere (*Sailing to Byzantium*).

However, a couple of miles away along the ridge above the Golden Horn is another ancient Byzantine church, St Saviour in Chora — literally 'in the country', for that is what it was when it was built, though it has long ago been swallowed up by city-spread. It too has suffered much over its fifteen centuries, was converted into a mosque, and is now a museum, but in spite of that, and partly because of its smallness and chiefly owing to the fortuitous preservation of its mosaics and frescoes, it is *not just an empty tomb but also a place of revelation*, one particular part of it especially so. This is the chapel along its south side, built as a mortuary chapel, a burial place — and therefore adorned with appropriate paintings of the Last Things: Death, Judgement, Hell and Heaven. And it is one of those paintings with which we are concerned.

It faces you fifty feet away at the east end when you enter the chapel. It is painted on the curved inner surface of the semicircular dome over the apse; and lest anyone should wonder what it's about, the unknown painter wrote upon it the initials *J. C.* and the Greek word *anastasis*, resurrection. The letters are quite small, but in clear white on a blue background — that deep, dark, luminous blue of the night sky when you first begin to sense that the dawn is coming. Framing that sky to left and right are rocks very pale in tone but contorted, split and shattered as though the artist had in mind St Matthew's description of what happened at the moment of Christ's death — the veil of the Temple rent in twain, the earthquake, the rocks rent and the graves opened.

Between those rocks, against that sky, and leaning slightly off-centre, is a large bright mandorla, that is, an oval surround to a whole body, as a halo is a circular surround to a head. This mandorla is rainbow-like in three bands — sky blue in the centre, pale blue next, and the outer band a shining white — and all scattered with golden stars. And in the middle of that bright oval the Christ — Christ who is stretching out his arms to left and right (I'll return to him in a moment) while beneath his feet against a grey-blue background are two gate-timbers and a chaotic litter of bits of metal — nails and bolts, the plates and pins and wards of all the locks of hell, and an almost invisible Satan lying prostrate beneath them.

In the middle distance of that broken rock landscape, and at either side of the picture, are groups of haloed saints; in the foreground, to left and right of Christ and just below him, are two stone tombs with their lids off and wide open. Out of one rises a white-haired, long-bearded man with a white robe over his blue undergarment. Out of the other rises a woman, also with a blue undergarment but her gown and hood are crimson. They are respectively — though perhaps we shouldn't immediately recognize them, for we generally imagine them to be more or less eternally naked — they are Adam and Eve, Man and Woman, the parents of us all — and as such they include us all. They each reach, and with yearning, a hand towards the dominant figure of Christ in the centre, that Christ who fills his bright mandorla with all its shining stars. He wears a voluminous ankle-length robe of a marvellous bright creamy gold bound with a broad sash of the same stuff, and thin enough to reveal the form of his strong legs which are planted wide apart to take the strain, the strain of raising Adam and Eve to lift them out of Death. His arms are outspread to them and their hands stretch up to him. But his hands have not taken their hands. No mere intertwining of fingers, no mere holding of hands will be sufficient to raise their weight, their dead weight. A more powerful grip is required for that — so he has got firm hold of Man and Woman by clasping their wrists. His whole being is movingly alive and alive with movement — and with superhuman grace and an unmistakable and flexed muscular power. And his face, with hair and short beard of reddish gold and ringed with a halo of pale gold, looks not at Adam, not at Eve, but down the whole length of the mortuary chapel at those who enter it, at ourselves as we look at this painting. His expression is not so stern as that on the face of some Byzantine Christs. But neither is it so soft as, for instance, the face of Christ painted in the Holy Sepulchre Chapel here. It is the face of One who is saying in so many words: 'You are all right. I've got hold of you. Come on and get up. Rise up and live with me.'

There's the picture which transforms the mortuary chapel of a church become a mosque become a museum into a place of unforgettable revelation. Firm in its drawing, rich in its colour, striking in design and dominated by that shining white Christ against a deep blue background and a landscape of shattered rock — with the ruins of sin and death littered about his feet, and Everyman and Everywoman gripped at the wrists by his mighty hands. 'You are all right. I've got hold of you. Come on and get up. Rise up and live with me' — or, in his words, as heard by St John on Patmos, 'Fear not. I am the first and the last, I am he that liveth and was dead, and behold, I am alive for evermore, and have the keys of hell and of death' (Revelation 1.17-18).

Istanbul is two thousand miles away. Moscow, South Africa, San Salvador — chilly, fearful names — are much further. But Ulster is much closer; Greenham Common, with all the fears it represents, closer still. But closest of all are the citadels of our own being, our own hearts. And so deadly the fear within them of that almost unmentionable five-letter word, Death, that the majority of our contemporaries feel imprisoned, powerless, and with less and less future to which to look forward. Dear people, if only we Christians will believe and trust in the Jesus Christ we have come to know something of over the years; believe and trust that he is indeed the conqueror, and has the keys of Hell and of Death; believe and trust his will and power to grip us by the wrists and lift us up into eternal life — what could we not do, what shall we not do, for him and for his world?

10

The Lord of the Dance

A Sermon for Easter Day [1]

*

Joy tickles the toes as well as the tongue. Always and everywhere men and women express it not only with singing but also with *dancing*. When a sovereign is crowned or a contest won, when good news comes or they fall in love, people don't willingly sit twiddling their thumbs or peeling potatoes. They sing and they dance. Age or infirmity or work-to-be-done may forbid the feet — but cannot forbid the heart to dance when human beings feel they're in step with the rhythms of the universe, with the music of the stars and with the dance of the atoms; when, if they be God-fearing men, they sense they are almost in step with God himself and with the pattern of purposes that he has ordained.

Don't be shocked by the suggestion that religion and dancing should go together. The Dance is the mother of most of the rites with which men try to worship God. The Israelites, Puritans as they were in some respects, were not ashamed to praise God's name in the dance. They danced on the beach of the Red Sea after their escape from Egypt. There was dancing when David had killed Goliath, dancing when the Ark was brought back to Jerusalem — and dancing, too, as well as music and fatted calf on that memorable occasion when a prodigal son came home; the only person who disapproved was that singularly unattractive character, the prodigal's elder brother.

[1]   April 1973

Symbols and Dances

In Christian times, too, men have praised God's name in the dance. There's not been much of it in Britain for the last three centuries. The British have been too ready to empty the Christian faith of its gaiety and joy, to narrow religion and make it no more than the grim groove of moral duty. But it was not so in the days of the apostles, and it was not so in the Middle Ages when it was not unusual to think of the Christian life as a Dance and of Christ himself as the Lord of that Dance. The carols men sang they also danced, and one of those carols represents the earthly life of Christ as a dance — that is, a pattern of ordered, graceful steps, a disciplined obedience to certain vital rhythms, a self-forgetting abandon to a pattern of movement ordained by his heavenly Father. It was at Bethlehem that Jesus joined in with mankind — to bring them out of their sinful confusion, back into step with God, back into the general Dance of the stars and the atoms and the angels. Sometimes the steps Christ footed as he went in and out among men were quick and gay, sometimes they were slow and solemn. But quick or slow, from start to finish his life on earth followed a pattern of graceful, courteous, rhythmic movement in concert with God and with such men as would be his partners.

But was it not only a Danse Macabre, a Dance of Death, ending — as so many of the sacred dances of primitive men ended — in a bloody and useless sacrifice? Most certainly the slow movement of Christ's Dance, the Pavane of his Passion, is not to be forgotten. When Christ came to dance with men he never sat out; he evaded nothing; he permitted Judas to kiss him, and he danced — as all men must — with death. BUT THE DANCE WENT ON: the Pavane of the Passion was not the end. For Christians believe, we honestly believe, that on the third day the tempo quickened, the step grew brisker, death had to let go — and Jesus was dancingly alive again and for ever.

Sydney Carter's modern hymn, *The Lord of the Dance,* is based on the medieval carol to which I referred just now:

The Lord of the Dance

I danced in the morning when the world was begun,
And I danced in the moon and the stars and the sun,
And I came down from heaven and I danced on the earth;
At Bethlehem I had my birth . . .

I danced on a Friday when the sky turned black,
It's hard to dance with the devil on your back.
They buried my body and they thought I'd gone;
But I am the Dance, and I still go on.

They cut me down and I leap up high;
I am the life that'll never, never die;
I'll live in you, if you'll live in me:
I am the Lord of the Dance, said he.

Christ does not dance alone. Others were involved. Only the exhibitionist wants to dance alone. Christ asked men to dance with him: 'Follow me', he said, and took great pains to teach them the steps. Some were too self-conscious or disapproving ever to take the floor. Some soon found the Dance he led them too demanding — and went and sat out. But others joined in with a kind of clod-hopping vigour. In their fishermen's boots they stumbled badly from time to time to begin with. But because they persevered grace gradually came — and their joy was unbounded when the partner they thought they had lost came back and held out his hands to them again. And few who read the Acts of the Apostles can escape the conclusion that they were the acts of men whose hearts were dancing whatever their bodies suffered as they went to the ends of the earth to bring others into the Dance. In the course of time those apostles also came to the Pavane and they too danced with death — but *because* they were still the partners of the dancing Christ they too came to their resurrection and to heaven. This, perhaps, is heaven: perfect life and perfect love, music and dancing, rhythm and melody, grace and courtesy, stars and atoms and beasts and flowers and men and angels — all with Christ, and Christ with God.

Now this is a way of looking at things which can have important, healthy and most liberating consequences for ourselves. For once we have committed ourselves to the belief that our lives are part of an ongoing movement of the whole creation, and that movement a Dance, then a great many things that bewilder us or dismay us will do so no longer. Once we accept that, in that Dance, there is no going back and no standing still, and that only those who are dead in heart or head can drop out — then we realize that it is senseless to make ourselves miserable grieving over the past and wishing the dance had stopped five or fifty miles back, five or fifty years ago. So we abandon ourselves to Christ's Dance in the spirit of which de Caussade wrote when he spoke of the Christian having a duty to abandon himself to the Divine Providence. And we are not to worry now about where the Lord of the Dance will lead us tomorrow — sufficient unto the day is the evil thereof. Dance one day at a time.

Dance one day at a time then, — out from God's house on Sunday, through the week's work in the world and back again next Sunday, and following the while the steps which Jesus has taught us and bringing others into the dance. Such a pattern of living is no grim groove of duty but a joyous dance if we've really appreciated what the resurrection means — that Christ danced *through* death. So to follow him demands some energy of heart, intelligence of mind, and suppleness of imagination; an ear for God's music and a sense of his rhythms; a fine sensitivity to what's going on and to the whereabouts of your partners' feet — so that you don't tread on any toes. It demands no little grace, which only Christ can give you, and the faith and patience to keep your balance in the slow and difficult movements. If we are solo exhibitionists, or acutely self-conscious, or lacking the confidence to abandon ourselves to where the Dance leads; and if we are sour, or superior, or censorious — then we shall probably prefer not to join in — and we shall have the prodigal son's elder brother for company

The Lord of the Dance

outside. But, in the words of the Psalmist, 'Let the children of Sion be joyful in their King. Let them praise his name in the dance' (Psalm 149.2-3).

11

Defending Ancient Springs

A Sermon in Springtime [1]

*

In his hymn *The Canticle of the Sun* St Francis of Assisi included this sentence: 'Praised be my Lord for our sister water, who is very serviceable unto us, and humble, and precious, and clean.' And although its relevance may not be immediately apparent I am going to ask you to think about our sister water and to go back to the fountain head of all things, the spring on which all life depends:

In the beginning the Lord God planted a garden eastward in Eden; and there he put the man whom he had formed . . . And a river went out of Eden to water the garden; and from thence it was parted and became into four heads. The name of the first is Pison: that is it which compasseth the whole land of Havilah, where there is gold; and the gold of that land is good: there is bdellium and the onyx stone. And the name of the second river is Gihon: the same is that which compasseth the whole land of Ethiopia. And the name of the third river is Hiddekel: that is it which goeth toward the east of Assyria. And the fourth river is Euphrates.

Time would fail to tell of Jordan and Jabbok, Kishon and Kedron; of the waterbrooks which the hart desireth and the waters of comfort that another psalmist sang; of the waters in which Jesus was baptized; of the waters of Jacob's Well of which Jesus said: 'Whosoever drinks of this water will thirst

[1]   May 1976

again: but whoever drinks of the water that I will give him shall never thirst . . . it shall be in him a well of water springing up into eternal life.' And when we get to the end of the Bible the spring is still welling and bubbling and he who is Omega as well as Alpha says: 'I will give unto him that is athirst of the fountain of the water of life freely.'

Well, yes — it's all very familiar. Too familiar, perhaps. We know all about water and usually take it for granted. We have only to turn our taps and out the stuff comes — clear and clean and cold. But we are less mindful of our springs and wells, all those small holes with which the surface of this planet is providentially perforated, and less mindful of the waters that well from them and run clear and clean and cold over the stones and through the cresses in brooks and streams and channels and conduits. We are apt to forget — or do not think it worth keeping in mind — that in at least four areas — in parts of Italy, in parts of Greece, in Persia and in Ceylon, areas which had been classic cradlelands of high civilization — things broke down and went backwards, and the quality of human living relapsed, because men had neither the will nor the energy to keep the streams and channels clean, so that the waters flowed ever more slowly, and gradually grew still in stagnant pools; and all was set for a mighty take-over of man by the anopheles mosquito, the bearer of malaria.

We are apt to forget — or do not think it worth keeping in mind — that our forefathers, from India in the east to Ireland in the west — told, and told again, a mysterious tale of a wounded King, of how by some strange consequence of his wound the streams throughout his kingdom ran low and began to dry up; and crops withered and animals died and the young men grew impotent and the young women sterile in a growingly gaunt waste land — until a hero brought salvation by freeing the waters — freeing them (according to the *Mabinogion* version of the story) when he had learnt to ask the right questions.

We are apt to forget — or do not think it worth keeping in

mind — all that springs and streams have meant to generations
of poets and prophets and seers and saints: the waters in which
nymphs and naiads bathed; the dark depths of our origins; the
deep wells from which truth has been drawn; the springs of
inspiration; the fonts in which we were baptized.

We are apt to forget — or do not think it worth keeping in
mind — the recent warnings of poets and prophets who have
spoken in our own century of these things: James Joyce
musing on the river Liffey; T. S. Eliot on the Thames and the
Mississippi; Vernon Watkins, taken up by Kathleen Raine,
affirming our need and duty to be 'defending ancient springs'.
Or, in a different vein, there has been David Jones writing of
priests still faithfully saying Mass at the sagging end and
chapter's close, between the sterile ornaments and the
pasteboard baldachins. Their garments are quaint by Mary
Quant standards; their congregations are usually small. But
they intend life as they continue to stand humbly before their
little altars, 'these rearguard details in their quaint attire,
heedless of incongruity, unconscious that the flanks are turned
and all connecting files withdrawn or liquidated — that dead
symbols litter to the base of the cult-stone, that the stem by the
palled stone is thirsty, that the stream is very low.' (*The
Anathemata*).

'Come off it', the plain-speaking, matter-of-fact, call-a-spade-a-
spade rationalist in us protests; 'this is codswallop. Twentieth-
century man has learnt to have a tin of Cerebos handy when
reading the outpourings of poets and prophets and seers and
saints; but when it comes to the real thing, he's no fool. He
knows what water is, and values it, and all that it really stands
for.'

We should not be too sure. Take these very straightforward
words from the introduction to a prosaic book of local historical
research published last year under the title *The Common
Stream*. The author, Rowland Parker, begins with these
words:

This is a true story. It tells firstly of a brook or stream, 'common' in the sense that it is but one of a thousand such streams which spring from the folds of hills everywhere, and especially in the chalklands of East Anglia. This particular stream rises a few miles to the southeast of Royston and meanders gently on a mere ten-mile course to join the River Rhee. In order to find it today you would need a large-scale map, and you would need to know exactly where to look for it . . . Even the local inhabitants are for the most part unaware of its existence. And having found it, you also would have some doubts; for in places the stream has been filled in and it flows, if at all, in an underground pipe. In other places it is so overgrown with nettles and reeds and tall grasses that you might well fall into it before you knew it was there. In yet other places, especially in a dry season, you could walk dryfoot along its bed for long stretches, as do the hares and pheasants. Only the willows mark its course with any real prominence, and even they, stricken by age and neglect, are fast disappearing . . . How can such a miserable stream, such a symbol of neglect and decay, have significance enough to merit its role as one of the principal threads of my story?

Part of its significance lies in that very fact, that it is a symbol of decay. Part lies in the very distant past . . . when every spring of water and every stream born of those springs was the object of veneration by groups of primitive men who knew, as surely and instinctively as the birds and beasts still know, though most men have forgotten, that the water of those springs and streams was Life itself.

If men today can so despise and neglect the springs and streams on which their bodies depend, how much more will they despise and neglect the springs and streams of living waters on which their minds and spirits depend?

Every generation has to face this major question: How much

should we be backward-looking to preserve to our use the good things we have inherited from the past? Or how much should we be forward-looking and change, even abandon, what we have inherited from the past in the interest of fairer things now and in the future? I used to believe, and still do believe, that the biblical answer is that it is better to fall for the future. Remember Lot's wife.

But I have come to think that the greatest service we can render at this present moment to those who will come after us is to set ourselves to the task of what Vernon Watkins defined as 'defending ancient springs'; and that our most urgent duty is not the further restructuring of the Church, the further contriving of its organic unity, the further up-dating of its liturgy or the further relaxing of its ethic — but defending the ancient springs, unstopping wells, cleaning streams, conserving conduits. The very fact that millions of human beings around us simply do not know what are the ancient springs to which I have referred — they include the Greek and Latin languages, the sagas of the Old Testament, the traditions of the origins of our peoples, the reservoirs of music written for use in the liturgy, as well as the classic formularies and rituals of the Christian faith — emphasizes the need. The swamps are daily extending here, the sterile sands advancing there. The wasteland daily grows. And those who, under God, will bring salvation will be those who, having asked the right questions, free the waters.

Having asked the right questions. For instance: What did Jesus mean when he said: 'Whoever drinks of the water that I shall give him shall never thirst . . . It shall be in him a well of water springing up into eternal life'? Part of the answer to the question lies in a formula more refreshing than the formula H_2O. This formula could have been a saying of Jesus, it could almost have come from St John's Gospel. In fact it is a short poem by the late Frances Cornford headed *Inscription for a Wayside Spring* and it could well be carved above the door of this and every church. Here it is.

ALL MEN FROM ALL LANDS
KNEEL BEFORE YOU GO
CUP YOUR HANDS
LIKE A BOWL
LET ME OVERFLOW
READ WHAT THESE WORDS TELL
LEAN DOWN AND KNOW
EACH ONE
BESIDE MY BRINK
BEND DOWN LOW
LOST SON
SAD DAUGHTER
BEND DOWN AND DRINK
I AM THE WATER OF THE WELL
THAT MAKES MEN WHOLE
I AM THE COLD WATER
THAT RESTORES YOUR SOUL

12

The Wind of the Spirit

A Sermon for Whitsunday [1]

✲

The Spirit, the Holy Spirit, is what Jesus had said he would send his disciples — and they were to go and wait in Jerusalem for it — or rather, for him. And wait they did. What they were expecting we do not know; probably they did not know themselves. But on the tenth day the Spirit came. 'They were all together in one place, when suddenly there came from the sky a noise like that of a strong driving wind, which filled the whole house where they were sitting. And there appeared to them tongues like flames of fire, dispersed among them and resting on each one. And they were all filled with the Holy Spirit and began to talk in other tongues, as the Spirit gave them power of utterance.'

That, in the words of the New English Bible, is how Luke described it. What they saw was something that reminded them of flickering flames; what they heard was a sound like the rushing of a mighty wind. The fiery aspect of the Spirit's nature I must leave on one side for another day; there is quite enough to be going on with if we confine ourselves this morning to thinking about the connection between this mysterious Holy Spirit and the wind.

It is probably safe to say that, though they didn't know what to expect, the apostles were not unprepared for something windy. They already connected 'wind' and 'spirit' in their minds. For those two English words there was only one Hebrew

[1] May 1970

word, and only one Greek word. And Jesus himself had suggested that there was some similarity between the wind and the Holy Spirit.

'The wind blows as it likes', he told Nicodemus, 'you hear its sound, but you can't tell where it comes from or where it is going. So is everyone that is born of the Spirit' (John 3.8). And bearing in mind that Christ's contemporaries knew nothing of electricity or radiation, we can appreciate why they should think that there was a similarity between the wind and the Spirit.

In the first place, the wind is invisible. It blows where it likes, and you hear the sound of it — but you can't tell where it comes from or is going to. Strictly speaking, you cannot even hear it — not the wind itself; you only hear the sound produced by something else when the wind strikes it — telephone wires, the rigging of a boat, windows that rattle, the door that bangs. Certainly we cannot see the wind. All we can see is the effect it produces — trees swaying, flags fluttering, smoke being blown from chimneys, and the sea being piled into great waves.

But although we cannot see it, the wind is real enough — and astonishingly powerful. In its more gentle and playful moods it merely blows the dust into our eyes and our hats off our heads. At other times it flattens crops, uproots trees, turns the calm sea of this morning into something frankly terrifying tonight. A typical hurricane in the eastern United States wrecked 26,000 motor cars, 20,000 miles of electric railway and 275 million trees. It has been estimated that the power of one such hurricane is equal to that produced in three to four years by all the dynamoes, turbines and other motors in the world.

But of all this power of the wind we make little use. We take it for granted that clouds will be brought to give us rain from time to time, and that they will then be blown away again that we may see the sun; that fogs and mists will be dispersed; that the air breathed by 30,000 people in Winchester today will be cleansed and freshened and changed before tomorrow — all this work of the wind we take for granted. For the rest, many city-dwellers would prefer a world without wind unless their hobbies are sailing or gliding. Certainly we do not exert ourselves to make any deliberate use of the great power of the wind. But it was not always so — our ancestors relied on the wind to get them across the seas, to pump the waters from the Fens, to grind the corn for their daily bread.

Why do we neglect this cheap source of great power today? For the obvious reason that the wind is so chancy and unpredictable — fresh and south-westerly today, almost imperceptible and easterly tomorrow. The wind bloweth where — and when — it likes. That is no use to us twentieth-century Westerners. Power we want, power we will have — but it must be power that we control, power we can rely upon, power we can switch on and off as we will to further our own desires and purposes. It is unthinkable that we should consent to live at the mercy and whim of the wind.

The wind is invisible; the wind is powerful; BUT the wind is unpredictable. It bloweth where it listeth, and thou hearest the sound thereof, but cannot tell whence it cometh and whither it goeth. So is everyone that is born of the Spirit.

No one can see the Holy Spirit. One can only see the effects, and hear the sounds, that he produces — lives of love and self-sacrifice and true holiness, words of unmistakable authority, inspiration and power. He spake, and speaks still, by the prophets; he worked, and works still, through the Saints.

And seeing and hearing these effects we begin to realize the immense power of the Holy Spirit, power that is mightily creative for good, but terrifyingly destructive of all that is false and flimsy. Simply recall the achievements of the apostles; of those who first brought the Christian faith to this island; of men like Michaelangelo, J. S. Bach, William Blake; of men like John Wesley and David Livingstone. Indeed the whole of history — and Christian history in particular — bears witness to the reality and power of the Holy Spirit, as does the Church's survival in the present century. When one considers all the forces arrayed against the Church today and our own tepid, unadventurous faith, our gross complacency, our divisions, our pride in the rightness of our own little views, our comfortable and uninspired daily existence, our dogged determination, that, come what may, nothing short of global catastrophe shall really be allowed to alter the way you and I have gone on living for the past twenty-five years — when one considers all this, then one wonders why the Church survives, until one realizes the immense power of the Holy Spirit.

Why do we not make more use of this power? We take it for granted that the solutions to our problems will turn up, that something will give us love and joy and peace and the other fruits of the Spirit, and do away with our sins — just as we take it for granted that something will disperse the fog, and bring us appropriate weather, and clear away by tomorrow all the stale air that goes in and out of our lungs today.

But further than this we hardly dare to go. The Holy Spirit of God, like the wind, is so unpredictable. We cannot control him. We cannot rely on him to be obedient to ourselves, to do the things we want done and to further our own pet schemes.

Dare we ask him to inspire us? To possess us? To fill us? To blow us along? Dare we let him decide what we shall say, or command what we shall do? Shall we not find it more comfortable, is it not more commonsensical and balanced and reasonable, not to risk it but to play for safety?

But are you sure you really know what safety is — and how to play for it?

13

The Rainbow round the Throne

A Sermon for Trinity Sunday [1]

*

One of the glories of this building is the great west window at the far end of the nave behind you. It is not what it was. Nobody can say for certain what it was, though it has been suggested that when it was created by Thomas, the glazier appointed by William of Wykeham six centuries ago, its subject was the Coronation of the Virgin. In December 1642 it was smashed to pieces by Cromwellian soldiers. After the pillagers had left the hundreds of fragments of broken glass were carefully gathered up, and when the King came to his own again at the Restoration they were put back as they are now — a great kaleidoscopic abstract through which the light pours with gleams and flashes of all the colours of the rainbow. Indeed, on a summer evening and with the setting sun behind it, it puts me in mind of that vision of that early Christian who, while interned on a Greek island, had the strange experience which he subsequently tried to put down on paper in what is now known as the Book of Revelation. He saw as it were a door open in heaven, and he heard a voice as it were a trumpet which told him to come up hither. And immediately he was in the spirit and 'there in heaven stood a throne, and on the throne sat one whose appearance was like the gleam of jasper and cornelian; and round about the throne there was a rainbow bright as an emerald' (Revelation 4.3).

It was an intensely colourful heaven into which St John was

[1]   June 1977

caught up — and there is something heavenly about all colour. Though often taken for granted, colour contributes much to our enjoyment of life in this world. Just think how much duller this world would be if everything were either black or white — no blue in sky or sea, no red in the sunset, no green in the grass, no gold in the ripe corn.

But now here is an odd fact: the Bible in general, and the New Testament in particular, is noticeably lacking in colour. There are, in the Authorised Version of the New Testament, over 180,000 words; but outside the Book of Revelation there are only twenty-seven words denoting colour. 'White' is the commonest; in one form or another it occurs just eight times; then comes purple — seven times; red, three times; black, three times; and two splashes each of gold, green, and scarlet. Of the two uses of the word 'green', however, one does not really denote colour at all, but translates a Greek word meaning 'full of sap'. The words 'brown' and 'yellow' and 'blue' never occur in the New Testament. Further, in almost every case such colour words as there are are used with reference to clothes; there are only two references to the colour of the landscape, only one to the colour of the sky, and none at all to the colour of the sea. It is not until we come to the Book of Revelation — written not in Palestine but on a Greek island — that the New Testament becomes at all colourful — and there is a rainbow round about the throne.

Why this lack of colour in holy Scripture — for what has been said of the New Testament is proportionately true of the Old Testament also? Three reasons may be suggested:

First, men in biblical times were simply not colour-conscious to the same extent as we are today — just as they were not much conscious of the natural beauty of the landscape. There was virtually no art of painting, and there is virtually no description of scenery in the Bible; men had no time to stop and stare, to notice and enjoy such things. The land meant hard work always, and danger often; it was thin pasture and scrubby hillside, stony field or battle field. Shepherds must watch their flocks by night and by day. If colour is noticed at all it is indoors, and particularly in clothing and precious stones — in Joseph's coat, in Solomon's glory, in the High Priest's breastplate, in the purple robe with which Jesus is dressed up by the Roman soldiery. For natural colour men had little eye.

Secondly: the climate of Palestine was — and is — such that the fresh natural colours of spring are quickly burnt up by the sun; thus the largely bald and stony countryside soon becomes, and for months remains, of a uniform, sun-scorched hue. There's no rich colourful summer, no golden autumn, no flaming fall. And that same heat which dries up the earth also dries up the air, so that there is none of that moisture-laden atmosphere which is so largely responsible for the brilliant colours of, say, the west of Scotland or of the Emerald Isle of Ireland.

The third, and perhaps the chief, reason why there is so little mention of colour in the Bible is the sheer all-pervading brightness of the light itself in the Holy Land. It was the intense luminosity of the sky above, and its hard, bright, sharp reflection off the surfaces of stone and rock on the earth beneath, which so impressed men — as it drained the landscape of its natural colours. This, rather than colours, was what men noticed — not the reds, yellows and blues of the spectrum, but the clear, brilliant radiance of the light itself — and, by contrast, the deep dark of shadow and cloud and night.

Now: it was that white intensity of the light itself through which the prophets and psalmists of Israel came to know so much of the nature of God, as it was through him who called himself 'the light of the world' that the writers of the New Testament came to know still more about him. Prophets and psalmists, apostles and evangelists — these were men of peculiar vision, men who saw behind and beyond all outward appearance to the ultimate reality, who saw (as it were) behind and beyond all colour to what is, in reality, the source of all colour — the pure light itself. They were men who glimpsed, so to speak, beyond the rainbow round the throne to him who sitteth upon the throne.

So, from Genesis to Revelation, it is the testimony of such men that God is light, and in him is no darkness at all. He dwells in light unapproachable, says one. Clothed in majesty and honour, he decketh himself with light as with a garment, says another. This is the light which blazed out at the dawn of the creation and is said to be the source of all life; this is the light which Moses saw in a bush in the desert and which Isaiah glimpsed in the Temple — a light so bright that the seraphim must veil their faces. This is the light which Peter and James and John saw in Jesus when he was transfigured before them; the light which blinded Saul on the road to Damascus. This too is the sharp brilliance under which the world is judged, which pierces the darkness and reveals all things and all men for what they are, which makes all things new, which gives illumination to them that sit in darkness and in the shadow of death, and guides men's feet into the way of peace.

Of colour, I repeat, the Bible seems to have little — but on page after page of it the world of men is seen under the pure light which contains all colour, the blinding light of truth, the light which probes and pierces men and women, which quickens them into new life, which bathes them with serene radiance. Light is, as it were, the visual expression of the splendour and glory of God, of the perfect goodness of God, of the aweful holiness of God.

'Stop', we cry, 'This is too much: we can't see all this.' It is too much. It is indeed. There have been many in the past, there are indeed men and women alive today, who have in fact experienced this illumination, and have seen all this in this light. It is a perfectly genuine and not uncommon mystical experience. But it is too much for the majority of us. As the hymn puts it, 'The eye of sinful man God's glory may not see.' It would kill most of us to see God now in all his naked and holy brilliance. We must have something between us and him, clouds and darkness round about him to temper the dazzle, a prism to split the glory of God into its myriad constituent colours. Even in heaven John saw a rainbow round about the throne.

And this is, in fact, how God in his mercy and understanding reveals himself to us — gleam by gleam, flash by flash, as precious stones splinter the light and give it to us gleam by gleam and flash by flash; as the great west window of this nave splinters the light and gives it to us in a sparkling kaleidoscopic diagram of all the colours of the rainbow. Once a year, on Trinity Sunday, we are to screw up our eyes to try to look for a blink into the heart of Light itself. But for the rest of the year, as the Sundays and weeks go by from Advent to Advent we are shown in the psalms, lessons, prayers, if we will but see them in the right way, one after another all the facets of God's being and activity in all their different colours — his power and imagination as Creator and Lord of History, his mercy and love in the life of Jesus, his sanctifying energy in the works of the Holy Spirit. And not only in our services of worship but at all times and seasons we can see splinters and flashes of the glory of God in the loving, caring, understanding words and deeds of the men and women around us — in the words of their mouths, the looks in their eyes, in the smiles on their faces, in the touch of their hands. And inasmuch as the words of *your* mouth, the look in *your* eyes, the smile on *your* face and the touch of *your* hand can reflect just a splinter of the glory of God, *you* too are — or could be — part of the rainbow round about the throne.

But just once a year, on this particular day, Trinity Sunday, we are to screw up our eyes, our courage, our minds, our imaginations, and we are to peer through a glass darkly through the rainbow round the throne to try to descry upon that throne the source of all light and the heart of all colour — the ineffable being of God himself. We are, in faith, to acknowledge the glory of the eternal Trinity, and in the power of the divine Majesty to worship the Unity.

> Immortal, invisible, God only wise,
> In light inaccessible hid from our eyes,
> Most blessed, most glorious, the Ancient of Days,
> Almighty, victorious, thy great name we praise.
>
> Great Father of Glory, pure Father of light,
> Thine angels adore thee, all veiling their sight;
> All laud we would render: O help us to see
> 'Tis only the splendour of light hideth thee.

14

God's Fireworks

A Sermon for All Saints-tide [1]

*

In days gone by the Book of Common Prayer contained a form of service headed 'Thanksgiving for the Nation's Deliverance from Gunpowder Treason and Plot', and today being November 5th we would be following that service instead of Morning Prayer. But it is a hundred and twenty years since Parliament decided it was no longer proper to do such a thing, and therefore struck the service out of the Prayer Book. In spite of which, for every one person who celebrated All Saints last Wednesday, there must be scores who are celebrating Guy Fawkes this weekend. It's not altogether surprising. Not everyone enjoys going to church, especially on a weekday in November. But however wet the grass, damp the air or cold the wind, fireworks round a bonfire are almost irresistible — fireworks in particular.

They are fascinating in their variety as they are exhilarating in their effect. There are those which make their chief appeal to the ear — the squibs and crackers and thunderflashes, whose glory is in their bang and of which we may say that they are of good report. Then there are those that are lovely and appeal chiefly to the eye: Silver Fountains and Golden Rain, Catherine Wheels and Roman Candles, Mines of Serpents and Bouquets of Gerbs — there is magic in their very names, but the magic of their names is nothing to the magic of their showers and torrents of sparks and stars. Above all there are

[1] November 1978

the rockets and shells, rushing up with a hissing trail of sparks and bursting into coloured constellations high above the darkened earth.

The variety is fascinating; the effect is exhilarating. Not invariably, of course. The modern firework owes its origin and development to the science and sin of war. The Very light over the battlefield, the maroons that announce the beginning and end of the two minutes silence on Remembrance Sunday, the rockets fired from ships in distress and to call out lifeboats — these may cause the heart to beat faster, but with fear or sorrow rather than with joy. Nevertheless, it is chiefly with occasions of rejoicing that we connect fireworks — notable anniversaries, the victorious ending of wars, or coronations, jubilees and other high royal occasions.

Fascinating in their variety, exhilarating in their effect, there is only one disease to which fireworks are liable — but that is quite fatal: dampness. The wet squib will not crack, the wet Catherine Wheel will not go round, the wet rocket will stay with its stick in the mud.

Whatever may have been the case in the Far East, fireworks were unknown in the Middle East in biblical times. Perhaps the nearest approach to fireworks in the New Testament is Peter's reference to an approaching persecution in his First Epistle; he calls it 'a fiery trial'. A few months later the expected persecution broke out. The Emperor Nero, perhaps just because he had no fireworks, was rumoured to have set fire to the thatched roofs of Rome. Alarmed by the reaction of the citizens, he quickly put the responsibility upon the Christians; and we have it on the good authority of Tacitus that the Emperor caused a number of those Christians, while still alive, to be dipped in tar, tied to trees and poles, and then set on fire to illuminate his gardens. The Roman citizens, like Tacitus, had no love for Christians, but both they and he were sickened by such calculated cruelty which used the followers of Jesus as human fireworks. And yet, in a terrible way, it was true. Those martyrs were Roman Candles. And it is not entirely unreasonable to suppose that, had the writers of the New Testament known what fireworks were, they would have likened the saints to them. Back in the Book of Wisdom its author had spoken of the righteous who shall 'run to and fro like sparks among the stubble'. Paul writing to the Christians at Philippi spoke of them as living 'in the midst of a crooked and perverse generation among whom ye are seen as lights in the world'. And Jesus himself, having just used a very homely metaphor in describing his disciples as 'the salt of the earth' and 'lights of the world', went on: 'Let your light so shine before men that they may see your good works and glorify your Father which is in heaven.'

Who are these like stars appearing? Who are the saints? Not only those whom Nero martyred, not only St Catherine on her wheel, but all the saints are the fireworks of God, fascinating in their variety, exhilarating in their effect. How bright these glorious spirits shine! How various they are! There is the goodly fellowship of the prophets; the prophets were those who, to put it crudely, made a bang — men who, by what they said and did, made people jump and sit up and take notice — men like Elijah, Isaiah and John the Baptist. And there is the glorious company of the apostles and there is the noble army of martyrs — apostles and martyrs, those saints whom we commemorate on certain particular days each year, men like Peter and Paul and Stephen and John, God's finest fireworks, rising like rockets from the darkness of the world and appearing like stars, high in the heavens, to whom ordinary men look up in wonder.

And there is that great multitude whom we commemorate at this season, All the Saints, some known, many unknown, men and women, of all sorts and conditions, as various as Catherine Wheels and Roman Candles, but one and all people who lived Christian lives of colour, crackle and sparkle. That is what distinguished them from the best of their good, respectable and pious contemporaries — the colour, crackle and sparkle of their Christian living. They ran to and fro like sparks among stubble. In the midst of crooked and perverse generations they were seen as lights in the world.

And as the saints are fascinating in their variety, so are they exhilarating in their effect. Who can read the true lives of the saints of the past — or meet a saint today — and not feel his heart beat faster? One and all, the saints are people who are fired with the love of God, let themselves go and allow themselves to be utterly burnt up and consumed for the sake of the glory of God, lighting up the darkness of the world around them. And the darker the world, the blacker the night, the brighter those glorious spirits shine, their whole lives spent unceasingly in celebration of the greatest of all victories and the highest of all royal occasions — the resurrection and ascension of the Lord Jesus. And whatever else we may say of them, we must say this of the saints — there is nothing damp about them.

'Let your light so shine before men that they may see your good works and glorify your Father which is in heaven.' We are not allowed to pretend that those words are only meant for a small hand-picked group of Christians in each generation. They are intended for all Christians. All, in Paul's phrase, are called to be saints. 'Let *your* light so shine' — not mine, or theirs, but yours. You are called to be saints. Fascinating indeed is the variety of ways in which, in the complex society of the twentieth century, Christians can fulfil the vocation of saintliness. That does not, of course, mean that God expects us all to take religious vows or become missionaries. Dons and doctors, nuns and nurses, students and secretaries, mothers and miners, pressmen and politicians — all can be saints. Some indeed in every generation are called, like the apostles and martyrs, to soar high into the sky; others are called to fulfil a prophetic function, to be Christians, who, by what they do and say, cause people to jump and sit up and take notice; but most of us are called to live our Christian lives in less spectacular ways, and in a simpler manner to shine with loveliness and to run to and fro like sparks among the stubble.

So to live is to give joy and happiness, to cheer and exhilarate the world, to cause men to catch their breath and look up and in the darkest of nights to rejoice in the greatness and majesty of God. But so to live means that we who are called to let our light shine before men today must at all costs avoid getting damp. The damp Christian, like the damp firework, has neither crack nor spark. Like salt that has lost its savour, he is only good for the rubbish heap. Yet it is so very easy to become damp and ineffective, and instead of creating joy to kill it. Too often, today as in the past, Christians cause the world to blaspheme rather than to glorify God, and cause it to blaspheme by being more concerned to censor such gleams of earthy joy as the world may have instead of outshining those gleams with the multicoloured sparkle of that heavenly joy which by God's grace they have it in them to show forth.

The good firework is not damp. It is dry as tinder, it is touched with fire, it lets itself go, and allows itself to be totally burnt up in producing that which is lovely and of good report.

Even so let your light so shine before men that they may see your good works and glorify your Father which is in heaven.

15

Monuments to Life

A Sermon for Remembrancetide [1]

*

Midway as we are between All Saints' Day and Remembrance Sunday I am going to ask you to think about a particular saintly church and a particular war memorial which share the top of a particular little hill in the Belfort Gap in eastern France — the gap which separates the Vosges and the Jura and links the great valleys of the Rhine and the Rhone. Throughout history it has been a highway for traders and pilgrims — and for armies. And just thirty-eight years ago this month, in November 1944, the Allied armies of liberation began to push eastwards through it to reach the frontiers of Hitler's Germany forty miles away.

The advance was desperately resisted, desperately slow, desperately costly of human life — and fighting was particularly severe on the little three-hundred foot hill overlooking the industrial township of Ronchamp. It changed hands several times. That hill had been recognized as a holy place from time immemorial, and for the last seven hundred years the small shrine of Our Lady at the top had been a famous place of pilgrimage. But in the fighting of late 1944 that church was reduced to rubble, and it was of that rubble that, in the 1950s, the great French architect Le Corbusier created a burial mound, a tumulus in the shape of a low pyramid, to be a memorial to those who had died in the fighting on that hilltop. Today that hill is visited by many thousands of pilgrims every year. But

[1]   November 1982

they do not go only, or even chiefly, to stand in silence beside that monument to the past; they go also, and chiefly, to visit another and greater monument on that hilltop — a *monument to the future* which in all ways overshadows, and is intended to overshadow, the burial mound, the monument to the past.

That second monument, also by Le Corbusier, has such power that it can be truly described as 'terrific', absolutely awesome. It draws people to it; it says something powerful to them; and they are sent by it. It is terrific, though it is only a pilgrims' shrine, only a tiny church. And you wouldn't know it was a church if the word 'church' suggests to you a piece of conventional religious architecture. It has neither dome nor spire, Romanesque arch nor Gothic flying buttress. Small in size — a mere eighty by forty feet, and with seating for only fifty and made entirely of rough concrete — it is still terrific. It draws people, says something powerful to them, and they are sent by it. The latest edition of the Encyclopaedia Britannica described it as 'the most important church of the past several centuries, so profound is its impact, so creative its force'.

How describe the shape of that small structure of dazzling white concrete which you see above you as you climb the hill? You can say there are three towers and four walls and a roof — but you have to add at once that there's little symmetry in the placing of the towers; that none of the walls is straight; that each has a different curve; and that the roof rises in an accelerating steep sweep up to one corner. Some might be reminded of a giant prehistoric cromlech with a single capstone perched at an angle upon upright monoliths; others might think of an upturned boat resting on the prow of a larger boat. But no such correspondence is intended, no symbolism to be looked for. Rather should the visitor be content to be drawn and captivated by the rhythms of different curves — curves that echo the natural slopes of the neighbouring hills and the undulating ridges of mountain and forest which bound the horizon in every direction; curves that are akin to the dynamic curves of the wings of aeroplanes and the bows of ships;

curves, above all, which are akin to those found in those instruments by which waves of sound and light are received and transmitted — the curves of mirror and lens and television screen, of radar equipment and satellite tracking apparatus and radio telescopes. This unique church, a monument on a battlefield, seems to look out over all Europe and into space, to open itself to the universe and to draw everything there is towards itself. And the nearer one gets the bigger the pull, the stronger the signals. It is Power that is being transmitted — not through a rhythm and pattern of words or music created by an inspired poet or composer, but through a rhythm and pattern of surface and curve created by the genius of an architect. As such, the signals transmitted can be picked up by all — irrespective of age or sex, of tongue or nation, of race or even of religion. To the Christian pilgrim they spell an answer to the psalmist's prayer: 'O send out thy light and thy truth that they may lead me, and bring me to thy holy hill and to thy dwelling.'

And what does the pilgrim see — and seeing, find — when he reaches the hilltop and enters the dwelling? At first very little. After the brightness of the wide sky without the light within is dim and muted. Apart from the glow of the votive candles all the light is natural, diffused and indirect. It comes down the shafts of the three towers and through the thick stained glass of the thirty to forty small windows of different shapes and sizes with which two of the thick walls are irregularly pierced. As the eye grows accustomed to this gentle and sincere light it begins to notice the curves of the roof, of the walls, of the sanctuary step; that the bare stone floor slopes *down* to the sanctuary; that the eight simple pews are all grouped on one side only and face the altar at an angle; that the altar itself is not in the middle but a little left of centre of the wall behind. Nothing in fact is symmetrical. Yet equally, if surprisingly, there is nothing disturbing in the fact. On the contrary, it is very largely by such means that the architect has created in so small an area an astonishing sense of space and of total tranquillity. The walls are all bare, rough-surfaced, off-white concrete. The only other objects to be seen are a cross standing to one side of the altar — and a little seventeenth-century figure of Our Lady standing quietly in a niche in the otherwise bare east wall; it is the only object that survived the devastating cataclysm of the battles in 1944.

When the architect handed over that chapel to the church authorities in 1955 Le Corbusier said that what had animated him and his fellow-builders had been a sense of the Holy. And he added: 'I have tried to create a place of silence, of prayer, of peace, of interior joy.' Any of you who has been there will know that it is indeed a place of those four priceless things — and it is so because it is animated, inspired, as its creators were, with a profound sense of the Holy. It stands on a small area of ground which, thirty-eight years ago this month, was churned up by a most bitter battle into a morass of mud and bone and blood. That that awful battlefield has been reclaimed and become for hundreds of thousands a place of silence and prayer and peace and interior joy is due to the fact that, under God, those who built it were men of faith in the future, men animated with a sense of the Holy and its power, men who built a pyramid mound as a monument to death and then went on to build a greater monument to life, that life which grows up out of death and sacrifice when men have faith in resurrection. In this monument on a twentieth-century battlefield all can meet a most powerful Presence — whatever their age, nation, race, even religion. To the Christian pilgrim that powerful Presence is the answer to the pilgrim's prayer: 'O send out thy light and thy truth that they may lead me, and bring me to thy holy hill and to thy dwelling' (Psalm 43.3). The prayer is answered, and the pilgrim hears a voice, as it were, saying, 'Be still and know that I am God.'

But then the voice adds: 'Whom shall I send?' This also the architecture of Le Corbusier's chapel at Ronchamp does. It sends its pilgrims. It sends them in the pop sense of the word, giving them an intense delight through its sheer and still beauty. But it sends them in a wider sense — as bearers of priceless things to others. Silence and prayer and peace and interior joy are not things to be kept in a handbag for one's own personal use and comfort. They need to be carried far beyond the hills of the Vosges and the Jura, into all Europe and beyond. The world is crying for these healing medicines. Whom shall I send with them? Where are the men and women who will not allow themselves to become petrified by wringing their hands over the loss of the past, but who will allow themselves to be sent out from this launching pad to carry silence, prayer and peace and interior joy to the ends of the earth? Who will carry far and wide the message of faith in resurrection, in life through and beyond death — that faith so powerfully transmitted over the countryside of eastern France by that unique war memorial on a twentieth-century battlefield?

Ronchamp is remote to you? Perhaps. But if you are a person of faith in life rather than in death, then you know you don't need to go to Ronchamp. You will know — if the truth has not become hidden from you by the fog of familiarity — that this Cathedral also says all that the Chapel of Notre Dame at Ronchamp says. From here too is transmitted an answer to the prayer, 'O send out thy light and thy truth that they may lead me, and bring me to thy holy hill and to thy dwelling.'

This Cathedral stands day in and day out that those entering it may find silence, prayer, peace and interior joy, and a Presence which says: 'Be still and know that I am God', a Presence that adds, 'Whom shall I send to carry this healing faith to others?' It should be our prayer that we may have the courage to answer: 'Here am I. Send me.'

16

The Cathedral

The Sermon preached on the author's
installation as Dean [1]

*

'No man can serve two masters', and a Christian's master is the
Lord Jesus Christ who uttered those words and who will judge
us all. Yet a newly hatched Dean may feel inclined to ask
himself whether he is not going to be required to do just that
— to serve two masters. To serve Christ, yes — and God help
me never to forget that; but there is the second master by
whom, it seems, a Dean's life is largely controlled, to whose
service he is bound by a solemn declaration, and for whose
safety and welfare he above all is personally responsible — and
that is the Cathedral itself. Many a writer has made this point,
T. S. Eliot among others. Just how imperious a master a
Cathedral can be was described in a grim novel by Hugh
Walpole half a century ago; and I take it that from now on,
whatever else I may or may not be and do, my days will be
chiefly ordered by the demands of this structure of stone, by
the sacred space this structure encloses, and by what goes on
within that sacred space. This is my master, as it is the master
of every one of us whose work is here. Yet no man can serve
two masters. How then can we serve Christ and serve this
Cathedral?

It depends of course upon what we think a cathedral is.
There are many definitions: a church in which a bishop has his
throne; the mother church of a diocese; a super house of God;

[1] November 1969

78

a monumental magnificence of medieval architecture; a museum; a mausoleum; a music hall; a 'must' for tourists. On a deeper level a recent writer on the subject, Albert van den Heuvel, has found it necessary to define a cathedral under fourteen heads — a sign of pro-existence; a symbol of diversity in unity; a Pentecostal laboratory; the theatre of basic drama; a temple of dialogue; a centre of creativity; an academy for committed information; a clinic for public exorcism; an international exchange; a broadcasting station for the voice of the poor; a tower of reconciliation; a motel for pilgrims; a house of vicarious feasts; and the hut of the shepherd.

For all their neo-religious jargon these fourteen points deserve the most careful study of any person who has to do with a cathedral; and I hope there will be opportunities in the future to say what I think they should mean and involve for us. But not this afternoon. Rather do I ask you to consider a definition that is both more simple and more profound, a definition made not of words but of rock, a definition given by one whom some consider the greatest European sculptor since Michaelangelo. By the kindness of the French authorities and of friends at Coventry Cathedral, and by the skill of printers here in Winchester, you have a photograph of Auguste Rodin's definition of a cathedral in your service paper. The man who knew the meaning of the Burghers of Calais, of the Kiss, of the Thinker, of Balzac, also knew something about cathedrals; he was passionately devoted to those of France; he visited them repeatedly; he recorded the impressions they made upon him in many notebooks and sketchbooks; and towards the end of his life he summed up everything he knew and felt a cathedral to be in those two marvellous hands. Why? The answer can only be gained and grasped by long contemplation of the sculpture itself, and for that you have to go to Paris; I hope a two-dimensional photograph will help; words fail, they simply won't do. But three clues may be suggested.

First: Rodin more often than not worked in bronze, but these hands are stone and they rise out of stone, out of a block of primordial rock, the elemental stuff of which every ancient cathedral is constructed, of which this great and marvellous building is made — this ancient fabric so cunningly constructed by builders, so lovingly preserved through the centuries, so steeped in the history of Wessex and of England, so treasured, so generously treasured, by the people of this diocese and city and by friends all the world over, so admired by so many visitors, and with which (if I may say so) I am more proud to be now associated than I can express. That is at the bottom of it all — of a cathedral as of everything else — elemental matter; and matter matters, whatever the lofty-minded and super-spiritual may say in their heretical moments. Matter matters.

But it is only the beginning. For secondly, arising out of the block of rock, growing up out of the material fabric which is what the outward eye sees and to which men normally confine the meaning of the word 'cathedral', Rodin saw something as soft as stone is hard, as animal as stone is mineral, as sensitive and creative as rock is inert — a pair of human hands. And it is to be particularly noticed that both hands are *right* hands. That is, they are the hands of two different and distinct human beings moving towards each other. But not for hearty handshakes, not to slap backs; still less to grapple, grab, filch, smite or slay. They are the hands of persons approaching each other, feeling towards each other, gently, caringly, lovingly, albeit with a certain proper shyness, as if both persons are sensitive to the fact that when it comes to drawing nearer to another human being one must be marvellously tender, infinitely patient and have endless respect for the other person's integrity.

If then we are prepared to learn of Rodin, this cathedral is very much more than its fabric, however marvellous its beauty and venerable its history. The space which it encloses and the precinct with which it is surrounded are to be *par excellence* a meeting point for different, and possibly differing, persons: for the Christians of the Diocese of Winchester; for the people of Basingstoke and the people of Bournemouth, for Channel

Islanders and commuters from Hampshire to London — yes, of course. But more than that — a meeting point for men and women, for young and old, for employer and employee, for citizen and countryman, for Church and State, white and coloured, for intellectual and mechanic, scientist and artist, for the antiquarian and the space-minded, for saint and sinner and every variety of Christian and non-Christian — a meeting point where, and through which, different (and possibly differing) persons may grow in understanding of each other, feel towards each other, gently, caringly, lovingly, albeit with a certain proper shyness, sensitive to the fact that when it comes to one human being drawing nearer to another there is required marvellous tenderness, infinite patience and endless respect for the other person's integrity.

But thirdly: look once more at the Cathedral as Rodin saw the cathedral. Those two hands suggest *devotion* — the growing devotion of two persons towards each other *and* the growing devotion of both of them together towards something infinitely greater beyond them; devotion in the old sense of deep prayer, and prayer thought of as the outward, onward and upward aspiration of human spirits towards a transcendent God whose love lures them to seek him, whose Son Jesus Christ shows them the way, and whose Holy Spirit urges and chivvies them to follow that way.

This above all a cathedral is or ought to be — the means whereby human beings, finding each other, and through finding each other, aspire together to find God through the medium of worship, that worship which it is the primary function of a cathedral to offer with unceasing regularity on behalf of all God's creatures. Given the climate and conditions of today I confess I do not think it is always easy to see how this supreme function can best be served: the Church has yet to discover how best to meet the requirements of the space age within the given limits of medieval architecture, how best to blend the old and the new, the formal and the free.

But of two things I am sure: first, that it should be the aim of us all here to see that whatever is said and sung and done in this place is as excellent as we can possibly make it — excellent in performance, and excellent in sincerity and truth. And secondly, it will help greatly towards the attainment of that excellence if each of you repeatedly recalls Rodin's vision of the cathedral, and if you see that one of those hands is yours. The other is the hand of your neighbour. It could also be, it should also be, the hand of Christ, to whom, with the Father and the Holy Spirit, be ascribed, as is most justly due, all might, majesty, dominion and glory, now and for evermore. Amen.

17

Christian Commemoration

A Sermon at an Office of Solemn Vespers
sung by members of the Benedictine Houses of
southern England to mark the Fifteen-Hundredth
Anniversary of the Birth of St Benedict [1]

*

From the second of the four psalms of this Office, Psalm
111, verse 4, *Memoriam fecit mirabilium suorum, misericors
et miserator Dominus.*

Or, as the Book of Common Prayer has it: The merciful
and gracious Lord hath so done his marvellous works: that
they ought to be had in remembrance.

Or, as the Jerusalem Bible translates it: He allows us to
commemorate his marvels: Yahweh is merciful and
tenderhearted.

We are come together today because, by his mercy and grace,
God allows us to commemorate one of his marvels in particular
— the birth fifteen hundred years ago of the founder of your
Order, that Saint Benedict but for whom the story of Western
Christendom would have been unimaginably different — and
indeed but for whom this very Cathedral would not exist in the
shape it has, having been built to be the church of a Benedictine
house. To ourselves, who in our Anglican secular and
establishment manner try to perform the *Opus Dei* here
morning and evening, year in and year out, it gives no small
pride and no little comfort to count ourselves as having some

[1]   April 1980

83

frail bond of kinship with St Benedict, as it also gives us
enormous joy that we have been allowed the opportunity to
welcome you all today and make it possible for this particular
celebration of yours to happen within these walls, within this
quire in which your forerunners sang Vespers for close on five
hundred years. Thanks be to God that he allows us to
commemorate his marvels.

To commemorate is something that gives delight to all men
everywhere. Even in an age when so many of our
contemporaries are impatient of tradition and its rituals, and
pride themselves on being altogether forward-looking, they
still like to mark anniversaries. Indeed, commemorations are
two a penny: in 1980 it is the fifteen-hundredth anniversary of
the birth of St Benedict; in 1979 it was the nine-hundredth
anniversary of the building of this Cathedral; in 1978 it was
the fiftieth anniversary of the birth of Mickey Mouse. And that
last fact should pull us up and make us examine ourselves, and
ask what it is we think we are really doing when we celebrate
an anniversary.

One of the most agonizing problems of our age — it is
doubtful if it was any more agonizing for Benedict in his age
— is the problem of our conflicting loyalties to the past and the
future. In deciding what we ought to do in the present, how
much weight should be given to the conservation of the works
and the wisdom we have inherited from our forefathers in the
past, and how much to the needs of those who will come after
us in the future? Looking back we see much that we believe to
be of high value — a stretch of unspoilt countryside of great
beauty, say, or the Tridentine Mass and the Book of Common
Prayer. But looking forward we see the need for a motorway
through that stretch of countryside or for a Series III Liturgy
in place of the Tridentine Mass and the Book of Common
Prayer. And when circumstances are such that we can no
longer maintain a Delphic moderation and keep our balance on
the fence, the whole weight of Christian Scripture tells us
which way to topple. As was briskly said: 'Leave the dead to

bury their dead', and 'Remember Lot's wife', Lot's wife who stopped to look back with regret at the passing of dear old Sodom and so became a geological specimen of monumental proportions. Remember Lot's wife.

But there's the rub. How can we obey this command of our Lord Christ? How can we remember Lot's wife, and what became of her because she looked back, without looking back ourselves?

It depends, of course, upon what we mean by remembering, and how we suppose our memories function and are meant to be used. Probably the most popular description would run something like this: we believe that the past is irrecoverable and all our yesterdays are dead and gone. But we can return to the past through exercising our memory upon our own experience and our knowledge of the experience of others. That is what remembering is — in the common view — and memory is the device whereby we are transported in heart and mind out of the present and back into the past. Whether or not we literally shut our ears and eyes to what is going on around us we become more or less unconscious of where we now are, the people we are with, the activity on which we are engaged and the problems and duties lying before us — and we are elsewhere with other persons at some time in the past — yesterday or centuries ago. Our attention is switched to, and remains fixed upon, experiences which have become matters of history — until something happens to cause us to pull ourselves together, switch off our memory, and get on with the business of living where we are in the present.

But there is another and fundamentally different way of making an act of remembrance. It envisages remembering, not as a looking back and a going back, but as a re-calling. Not as a leaving of the present in order to return to the past, but as a bringing back of the past into the present — and in such a way that what the world regards as dead and gone is alive and with us and having a quickening and practical effect upon our thinking here and now, today and tomorrow.

To remember in this second manner requires considerable imagination and effort of will. It is so much easier to remember in the nostalgic manner first described and to enjoy a lovely wallow in a supposed golden age fifty or fifteen hundred years ago. So to remember nostalgically requires nothing of us — no present response, no reconsideration of our plans or priorities, no action in the here and now of today; so to remember is thus without effect — save, in the long term, the fossilizing effect upon ourselves that it had upon Lot's wife. But, to recall and bring back what is past and those who are no longer with us in the flesh into the present, and so re-presenting them — this can have most powerful, even miraculous consequences.

It is such consequences that our Office this afternoon, and every Office, and pre-eminently every Mass, can effect. For this Office, every Office, and pre-eminently every Mass, is a commemoration of his marvels which God of his mercy allows us — a commemoration, an anamnesis, a re-presenting: first and foremost of Christ himself; but also, through Christ and in Christ, of others:

— of St Benedict himself;
— of those disciples of St Benedict whom David Hugh Farmer and the Abbot of Quarr with their collaborators have so brilliantly evoked in a splendid commemorative volume just published;
— and, too, of all our Benedictine forerunners, not forgetting those who performed the *Opus Dei* daily for nearly 500 years in this very space.

And out of it all, out of this Office, so worthily and humbly and lovingly offered this afternoon, who knows what life-enhancing power will be released to inspire, strengthen and unite us? Who knows what miracles will come of it?

I end with a paragraph from one of the books of Helen Waddell, that fine scholar who had so great an appreciation of, and sympathy for, the saints and scholars of the cloisters of medieval Christendom:

Medieval Latin poetry read in these days has something of the quality of the 11th Chapter of the Epistle to the Hebrews: 'These all died in faith, not having received the promises . . . that they without us should not be made perfect.' If there is melancholy in the realization that the wisdom and kindness of mankind has profited the world so little, it is that we are still in Newton's square box of a universe; that Boethius' definition of eternity 'the possession of all time, past, present and to come . . . in one single moment here and now' is seldom hazarded in our experience. Yet by these things men live, and in them is the life of our spirit. (*More Latin Lyrics*)

Thus God allows us to commemorate his marvels. Truly he is merciful and tenderhearted. The merciful and gracious Lord hath so done his marvellous works that they ought to be had in remembrance.

To him, one God in three Persons, Father, Son and Holy Spirit, be ascribed as is most justly due all might, majesty, dominion and glory, now henceforth and for ever. Amen.

18

Importance in Miniature

A Sermon at a Service in Commemoration
of Jane Austen [1]

*

Eight years ago almost to the day I gave an address on the occasion of the unveiling of a memorial to Jane Austen in Westminster Abbey, and I am grateful to the Jane Austen Society not only for asking me to speak again but even more for suggesting that I repeat what I said then. In substance that is what I am going to do.

Our celebration of the two-hundredth anniversary of her birth in this, the place of her burial, has been deliberately played in a low key and with a minimum of fuss. She would, I believe, appreciate our reticence, as she would appreciate the reticence of the inscription on the memorial in Westminster Abbey — just two words JANE AUSTEN. She once asked, and would surely still be asking were she our contemporary: 'What is become of all the shyness in the world?' But if you want something rather more fulsome the inscription on her gravestone in this Cathedral will gratify your wish:

The benevolence of her heart,
the sweetness of her temper, and
the extraordinary endowments of her mind
obtained the regard of all who knew her, and
the warmest love of her intimate connections.

[1] December 1975

Their grief is in proportion to their affection,
they know their loss to be irreparable,
but in their deepest affliction they are consoled
by a firm though humble hope that her charity,
devotion, faith and purity, have rendered
her soul acceptable in the sight of her
REDEEMER

Such language is too cold and at the same time too cloying for twentieth-century taste; for something more warm and matter-of-fact listen to her own opinions of aunts and apple tarts and miniskirts recorded in her letters:

'Now that you are become an Aunt you are a person of some consequence . . . I have always maintained the importance of Aunts as much as possible.'

'I am very glad the new cook begins so well. Good apple pies are a considerable part of our domestic happiness.'

'You will find Captain — a very respectable, well-meaning man, without much manner, his wife and sister all good humour and obligingness, and I hope . . . with rather longer petticoats than last year.'

There are some who consider the status of an aunt to be a small matter, and most of us consider apple pies and petticoats to be small matters — but those quotations are given with a purpose: to focus attention on particulars, on little details. There is another letter of Jane Austen's written on 16 December 1816, her forty-first and last birthday. In it she congratulates her nephew on leaving school, on getting away from Winchester, and goes on to defend herself against the mock charge that she has pilfered his manuscripts: 'What should I do with your strong, manly, spirited sketches full of Variety and Glow? How could I possibly join them on to the little bit (two Inches wide) of Ivory on which I work with so fine a brush . . .?'

That sentence has often and justifiably been picked upon as a most illuminating comment upon those novels which are her real memorial. Each is a little bit (two inches wide) of ivory worked with a fine brush. The details are minute and perfect, and the whole is confined within the narrow limits which she herself described as 'human nature in the midland counties'; and again, and even more precisely, as '3 or 4 Families in a Country Village'. In that small, green and pleasant land in which her characters lead their lives there is not one satanic mill. In those novels there is no violence, there are no deaths. In her lifetime the Industrial Revolution progressed at an accelerating speed till it was come to the dawn of the Railway Age; in her lifetime the French Revolution happened and the Napoleonic Wars were fought. But her novels are innocent of all reference to those turbulent events. Nevertheless, as Lord David Cecil has remarked in his introduction to the World Classics edition of *Sense and Sensibility*:

> On the minute stage of her genteel comedy theatre for daughters of gentlemen she presented the struggle that was rending intellectual Europe. Consciously or not, in Elinor is embodied all the philosophy of Dr Johnson, in Marianne all the philosophy of Rousseau . . . The visible structure of Jane Austen's stories may be flimsy enough; but their foundations drive down deep into the basic principles of human conduct. On her bit of ivory she has engraved a criticism of life as serious and as considered as Hardy's.

The same point has been made again by Mr Tony Tanner in his introduction to the Penguin edition of *Mansfield Park*:

> If (as has just been made clear) Jane Austen could see that a world of frantic change was about to supplant the world of peaceful fixity she knew, why then does she allow the spirit of Mansfield, in the figure of Fanny, to triumph over the forces of change, as exemplified by the Crawfords? I think one could put it this way. To a world abandoning itself to the dangers of thoughtless restlessness, Jane Austen is holding

up an image of the values of thoughtful rest. Aware that the trend was for more and more people to explore the excitements of personality, she wanted to show how much there was to be said for the 'Heroism of principle'. It is a stoic book in that it speaks for stillness rather than movement, firmness rather than fluidity, arrest rather than change, endurance rather than adventure. In the figure of Fanny it elevates the mind that 'struggles against itself', as opposed to the ego which indulges its promiscuous potentialities. Fanny is a true heroine because in a turbulent world it is harder to refrain from action than to let energy and impulse run riot . . . Jane Austen was aware of an England that was passing away. She knew about the passion which turns to lechery, the activity which becomes destructive, the energy which results in the collapse of a world. And . . . she appreciated the value of 'the quiet thing', and knew, too, the incredible moral strength required to achieve and maintain it. And that, above all, is what *Mansfield Park* is about.

Well, there is matter there for many sermons. But let us keep to the little piece, two inches wide, of Ivory. In the opening chapter of his book *The Savage Mind*, the French social anthropologist Lévi-Strauss digresses from his examination of the nature and functions of myths to draw attention to the fascinated delight many of us take in *small-scale models* — from doll's houses and Dinky toys, ships in bottles and Japanese gardens, up to the miniatures of a Holbein or a Hilliard and the paintings of those Dutch and Flemish artists who delighted to paint such tiny details that they must have used a magnifying glass to paint them as we need a magnifying glass to see them. Lévi-Strauss suggests that the small-scale model or miniature is the universal type of the work of art. All miniatures seem to have an intrinsic aesthetic quality — and whence do they draw this virtue if not from the dimensions themselves? — and the vast majority of works of art are small scale, are reductions from full size. And it isn't just a question of economy in the use of materials. There appears to be some inherent virtue in reduction itself. In Schumacher's now classic phrase, small is beautiful. A small-scale model enables a man to acquire straight away some understanding of a thing *in its totality*. If we want to understand something the usual procedure, the scientific procedure, is to dissect it, to take it to bits. We divide to conquer, we analyse to understand. But a miniature or model gives us the whole in small scale from the outset, and leaves us to work up to full scale as and when we can, leaves us free to use our imaginations to enlarge the picture until it embraces (as it will if it has been truly and faithfully made) not only the original large as life but much else besides — as the Lady Julian of Norwich could see the cosmos in a hazel nut; as Blake could see a World in a grain of sand and a Heaven in a wild Flower. In the same manner, because they are miniatures truly and faithfully drawn with a fine brush by a superb artist, the novels of Jane Austen can show us much much more than three or four families in a country village in the midland counties. We can see in Mansfield Park not only a picture of all England in 1814 but also a picture of all the world in 1975 — and it can give us strong intimations of heaven and of hell.

Indeed, it is through miniatures and models that most of us have come to possess what we have of eternal truth. What else but little bits of ivory two inches wide worked on with a fine brush are the myths with which the Bible begins and ends? Above all, what else are the parables of Jesus of Nazareth? Both myths and parables are drawn within tiny limits, and both are made up of apparently small matters — if not aunts and apple pies and miniskirts, certainly fruit trees and fig leaves, bridesmaids and oil lamps, trusty servants and lazy servants, sheep and goats, even so small a thing as a mustard seed. But such miniatures have infinite connections. And if only we would learn that small is beautiful, and if only we weren't so fond of taking things to bits, we should understand the same of much else besides — that they have infinite connections; we should understand what Luther meant when he said: 'If you want to see the holy Christian Church painted in glowing colours and in a form which is really alive . . . you must get hold of the Psalter'; we should better appreciate Gothic cathedrals and Byzantine churches which were deliberately built to be microcosms, small scale models, of the universe; we should better observe and experience Sunday, as Sunday is intended to be observed and experienced, as a miniature experience of heaven; and we should more easily recognize what Jane Austen called 'The Sacrament' to be what it really is — a miniature of heaven: nature, man and God united in perfect communion and wholeness.

To begin to see such things, so much in so little, and thus to be called to enter into the joy of our master, it is required of us that we be *faithful over a little* — and being faithful over a little involves quietness and patience and a certain self-effacing reticence and modesty that Jane Austen would have called 'shyness': 'What is become of all the shyness in the world?' Being faithful over a little involves not being noisy and blasé and falling for the big and the brassy; not disdaining little things; not despising things near at hand, things apparently so ordinary as to be beneath our notice. Being faithful over a little involves, rather, seeing in those very things — the little things, and those near at hand, and those apparently ordinary — the basic materials and proportions of the Kingdom of heaven. For the Kingdom of heaven is as a grain of mustard seed. Small is beautiful. Julian of Norwich saw all heaven in a nut; Blake saw it in grains of sand and in widlflowers; Jane Austen saw it in human nature in the midland counties.

> Where in life's common way
> With cheerful feet we go;
> Where in his steps we tread
> Who trod the way of woe;
> Where he is in the heart,
> City of God, thou art.

Symbols and Dances

Not throned above the skies,
Nor golden-walled afar,
But where Christ's two or three
In his name gathered are,
Be in the midst of them
God's own Jerusalem.

19

Study to be Quiet

A Sermon at a Service in Commemoration of Izaak Walton [1]

*

And he showed me a pure river of the water of life, clear as crystal. (Revelation 22.1)

The day is far spent (and has been hot) and I must be brief — and inevitably Izaak Walton will get less than he deserves; much that should be said will remain unsaid. But then you already know it — the Stafford child, the London ironmonger, the friend of divines, the author of *The Compleat Angler* and the maker of five exquisitely cut jewels of biography; a man particularly associated with Winchester, with its Close that became his home, its Cathedral in which he worshipped and lies buried, its river on whose banks he studied to be quiet.

His were not days when quiet was easily come by: they were days of Plague and Fire; of intense and hateful controversy not only in politics but also in religion; of war, and what is much worse, civil war; of Gunpowder Treason and Plot; of the deliberate smashing of much beauty, not least in this Cathedral — not to mention the defeat, the capture, the trial and the execution of the King.

But out of all that emerges this man Izaak Walton who, though he held strong opinions both as a Royalist and a High Churchman, was a man of wide sympathy, of sincere and simple piety, of deep appreciation of the beauties of nature and

[1] July 1983

95

all the blessings of this life, and above all, of great gentleness and of singular charm and charity. And if, as he certainly did, he owed these and his other virtues to the grace of God, and owed them too in some measure to the company of the good men who were his friends, I am convinced his loveable character was also much shaped by *rivers* and his quiet study of their music and movement and of all that went on in their clear streams and in the water meadows and little villages and towns through which they flowed. I cherish the thought and tradition that he spent hours in meditative thought beside that little branch of the Itchen that still flows through the Close here — and would that we all had the leisure to do the same. We should be saner and saintlier than we are.

But, alas, the Itchen today flows unregarded by most people most of the time. It has no obvious connection with what comes out of our taps; as a boundary it has ceased to matter; its economic value is small; it turns few mill-wheels; it can no longer carry stone, corn and coals to Winchester's wharf. But regarded or not, it still runs, and very equably, modestly, subtly and surely helps to shape the lives of those who live in its valley. It waters our meads and gardens, gives us both mists and mellow fruitfulness, and beside it, if we will, we can still find what Walton found — healing and re-creation.

It is, no doubt, their power to heal and re-create unquiet men with unquiet minds that has made rivers such an attraction for men. Artists love them, and running water, clear and clean and making a music to match its motion, is perhaps the most elemental stuff of which poetry is made. From Homer and Virgil right down to our own day sweet streams have run softly through the literature of Europe — and of Britain in particular. Nymphs and naiads, which earlier poets used to see, are now exceedingly rare; they don't like the noise and smell of motors, nor do they fancy bathing their bright bare bodies where the clean gravel and waving weed are fouled with tin cans, polythene bags and suchlike ugly garbage. Nevertheless the river still runs as it did in Walton's day, as it did before the Normans came, before the Romans came, as it did right back in those prehistoric times when (in the words of Rowland Parker in his book *The Common Stream*) 'every spring of water and every stream born of those springs was the object of veneration by groups of primitive man who knew, as surely and instinctively as the birds and beasts still know, though most men have forgotten, that the water of those springs and streams was Life itself.'

The river of life still runs, as it runs in a silvery stream through the whole length of holy Scripture (we heard of it in that Lesson from Ezekiel) from the second chapter of Genesis, where it has its spring in the Garden of Eden, to the last chapter of Revelation where in the holy city, New Jerusalem, an angel showed St John 'a pure river of water of life, clear as crystal, proceeding out of the throne of God and of the Lamb . . . and on either side of the river was there the tree of life, which bare twelve manner of fruits . . . and the leaves of the tree were for the healing of the nations.'

It was by such waters that Izaak Walton studied to be quiet. Out of such studies emerged *The Compleat Angler,* and — I repeat — it is my conviction that, under God, it was from those studies by those waters that he derived his nobility, his simplicity, his contentment, his pellucid goodness.

But, and this has to be added in conclusion — there is another River — or rather, the same River seen from another angle — not the river viewed by man the onlooker standing on the bank and watching its water flow past at his feet, but the river known by man as *part of it,* floating and flowing with it, carried by it — the River of Time which like an ever-rolling stream bears all its sons away, as it bore Izaak Walton three hundred years back and will bear you and me less than three hundred years ahead. This raises solemn questions related to those churches, monuments and charnel houses of which we heard earlier: questions like — How far in its development, *and ours*, has this River of Life and Time come? And where is this River carrying us? And so I give you these lines of Matthew Arnold:

> This tract which the river of Time
> Now flows through with us, is the plain.
> Gone is the calm of its earlier shore.
> Border'd by cities and hoarse
> With a thousand cries is its stream.
> And we on its breast, our minds
> Are confused as the cries which we hear,
> Changing and shot as the sights which we see.
> And we say that repose has fled
> For ever the course of the river of Time.
> That cities will crowd to its edge
> In a blacker, incessanter line;
> That the din will be more on its banks,
> Denser the trade on its stream,
> Flatter the plain where it flows,
> Fiercer the sun overhead.
> That never will those on its breast
> See an ennobling sight,
> Drink of the feeling of quiet again.
>
> But what was before us we know not,
> And we know not what shall succeed.
>
> Haply, the river of Time —
> As it grows, as the towns on its marge
> Fling their wavering lights
> On a wider, statelier stream —
> May acquire, if not the calm
> Of its early mountainous shore,
> Yet a solemn peace of its own.

And the width of the waters, the hush
Of the grey expanse where he floats,
Freshening its current and spotted with foam
As it draws to the Ocean, may strike
Peace to the soul of the man on its breast —
As the pale waste widens around him,
As the banks fade dimmer away,
As the stars come out, and the night-wind
Brings up the stream
Murmurs and scents of the infinite sea.

For Arnold that was the end. It was not the end for Izaak Walton — and it isn't the end for us who share his faith.

The last end is in that heavenly city, New Jerusalem, where the angel will show us a pure river of water of life, clear as crystal, proceeding out of the Throne of God and of the Lamb . . . and on either side of the river is there the tree of life which bears twelve manner of fruits — and the leaves of the tree are for the healing of the nations.

20

At the End of a Festival [1]

It's end of term, the Festival is nearly over, and

> The time has come, the preacher said,
> To talk of many things,
> Of bugs in beds, and Gustav Holst,
> Of woodwind, brass and strings,
> Of Scottish reels and liturgy,
> Gethsemane and stings.

I'll leave the bugs in their beds for minute or two, and the stings must wait to where they belong — in the tail. For the moment, think back four evenings, to the very beginning of this Southern Cathedrals Festival, the performance of Holst's *Hymn of Jesus.* It was not a work I'd ever heard — but I was captivated by the music — and no less by the text Holst used. In fact he used two: first, the great sixth-century Latin processional hymn composed by Venantius Fortunatus for the coming to a nunnery in France of a relic of the True Cross.

> *Vexilla regis prodeunt,*
> *Fulget crucis mysterium.*

> The royal banners forward go,
> The cross shines forth in mystic glow.

The second text Holst took from *The Acts of John,* written in Greek and somewhere at the eastern end of the Mediterranean

---

[1] July 1984

about the year 200 AD. Like other lives of saints written in subsequent centuries, it was compiled with great imagination and not much regard for literal truth. Just as a later writer brought together and imaginatively embroidered stories of holy Swithun told in the streets of Winchester — of how he mended broken eggs and so on — so the unknown author of *The Acts of John* brought together and embroidered the tales told in the streets of Ephesus of a man who had been that city's bishop, the same John, it was believed, who had been the beloved disciple of Jesus, the author of the Fourth Gospel and the man who had seen the visions described in the Book of Revelation. Some of the embroidery is obvious embroidery — like the story of how, when going round his diocese, John and the members of his staff put up one night at a poor inn and the Saint got so irritated by the bugs in his bed that he said: 'I say unto you, O bugs, behave yourselves, and leave your abode for this night and keep your distance from the servants of God.' For the rest of the night John slept in peace, 'and in the morning there was seen a great number of bugs standing at the door of the house, and John looked at them and said: "Since ye have well behaved yourselves in hearkening to my rebuke, come unto your place." And when he had so said, the bugs, running from the door, hasted to the bed and climbed up by the legs thereof and disappeared into the joints. And John said again (and here's the sting in this tale): "These creatures hearkened unto the voice of a man, and abode by themselves and were quiet and trespassed not; but we which hear the voice and commandments of God disobey and are light-minded: and for how long?" '

Rebuke of our light-mindedness taken. Let us be more serious. A few pages further on the author records a series of incidents purporting to be John's own reminiscences of the days when he had been a disciple of Jesus. And this was one of them: at the end of the Last Supper Jesus 'gathered us all together and said: "Before I am delivered up let us sing an hymn to the Father, and so go forth to that which lieth before us." He bade us therefore make as it were a ring, holding one another's hands and himself standing in the midst he said: "Answer Amen to me." He began then to sing an hymn' — and the text of that hymn is what Holst used for the greater part of his Op.37 and which explains the title he gave it. The Last Supper is over . . . 'and when they had sung an hymn they went out to the Mount of Olives.' (Mark 14.26). And to the unknown Greek who wrote *The Acts of John* the word hymn meant much more than a congregational song of praise. It meant a ritual performance, a dance, a liturgy sung and danced to the glory of God, eleven disciples forming a ring, holding hands, dancing round and answering 'Amen' in response to the song of the Lord of the Dance in the centre. And I pick out these lines in particular:

Glory be to thee, Father. *Amen.*
Glory be to thee, Word. *Amen.*
Glory be to thee, Holy Spirit. *Amen.*
Glory be to thy Glory. *Amen.*
We praise thee, O Father; we give thanks to thee. *Amen.*
Divine Grace is dancing, fain would I pipe for you. Dance ye all. *Amen.*
Fain would I lament, mourn ye all. *Amen.*
The Heavenly Spheres make music for us. *Amen.*
The Holy Twelve dance with us. *Amen.*
All things join in the dance. *Amen.*
Ye who dance not, know not what we are knowing. *Amen.*
Give ye heed unto my dancing, for yours is the passion of man that I go to endure. *Amen.*
Fain would I move to the music of holy souls. *Amen.*
Know in me the word of wisdom. And with me cry again Glory to thee, Father. *Amen.*
Glory to thee, Word. *Amen.*
Glory to thee Holy Spirit. *Amen. Amen.*

The full text of the hymn as Holst used it you can read and study for yourselves on page 23 of the Festival Programme, or in M. R. James, *The Apocryphal New Testament.*

He invites us to join in his dance. A dance — be it a sophisticated ballet or a homespun Scottish reel or a liturgy of the Church (for all liturgies have their origin in dance) — a dance is a pattern of ordered and rhythmical and beautiful movement; and every step a Christian takes in his daily life is (if he will but see it and keep in step) a step in that universal dance of which Christ is the Lord. The Liturgy of the Church — this service in which we are this morning engaged — is the formal outward expression of the ever-ongoing joyous dance of Christ's Body. And the function of church music is no more and no less than to order, inform and inspire the rhythmical movements of our souls and bodies that we may dance our part in Christ's dance that much the better, with more glory to God and joy to ourselves and all concerned — and with less damage to the toes of our partners.

But then there is the sting in the tail. When they had sung an hymn they went out to the Mount of Olives — and you will remember what happened then, how the disciples broke away from the Dance and fled while the Lord of the Dance danced on alone — moving with grace through passion, crucifixion and death — and on to resurrection.

> I danced on a Friday when the sky turned black;
> It's hard to dance with the devil on your back.
> They buried my body, and they thought I'd gone;
> But I am the Dance and I still go on:
>
> They cut me down and I leap up high;
> I am the life that'll never, never die;
> I'll live in you if you'll live in me;
> I am the Lord of the Dance, said he.
>
> Dance then wherever you may be;
> I am the Lord of the Dance, said he,
> And I'll lead you all, wherever you may be,
> And I'll lead you all in the Dance, said he.

(Sydney Carter: *100 Hymns for Today*)

The last four days, and the music made in them, have set us all dancing with delight. We have known the Lord's Dance, and been caught up in it. And this Liturgy sums it all up. The Lord is bidding us 'make as it were a ring, holding one another's hands', and himself dancing in the midst and bidding us answer 'Amen' to his unending hymn to the glory of God. And when it's all over, and completed in Evensong this afternoon, then, when we have sung a hymn, we shall go out.

To what? To break away, leaving the royal banners to go forward alone, leaving the Lord of the Dance to dance on without us?

Or shall we not rather try to keep on dancing in the rhythm and steps of our Lord wherever he leads us? Wherever he leads us: we know little of what will befall us. However we do know this: that Festivals don't last for ever this side the grave, and that tomorrow will be Monday again. But the Dance will go on notwithstanding; and, please God, we shall hear in the morning of every day to come until our lives' end, the Lord saying to us: Let us sing an hymn to the Father, and so go forth to what lieth before us. Make as it were a ring, hold one another's hands and answer 'Amen' to me:

> Glory to Thee, Father. *Amen.*
> Glory to Thee, Word. *Amen.*
> Glory to Thee, Holy Spirit. *Amen. Amen.*